"Prayer is a distin[ct...]
It is also one of t[he...]
lives. *Without [God...]*
helpful, practical, and personal book that will help you
live a more faithful and vibrant life of prayer and be a
more faithful disciple. This book brings some of the
giants of prayer to the reader in such a practical way. The
author makes this book intensely personal because he is
a man of prayer and he is a man who has sought the
presence of God throughout his life. Read this
book. Teach this book. Delight yourself in the truths this
book presents and you will treasure even more the
presence of God."
— Mark McClellan, J.D.; Ph.D. Ethnic Evangelism Specialist,
Baptist General Convention of Oklahoma; Professor of Christian
Studies, Oklahoma Baptist University

"My former missionary colleague, Dr. Dennis Davidson,
offers us keen insights into the theology and practice of
prayer. Written by one who obviously both understands
the dynamics of prayer from a scriptural perspective and
from lessons learned as a devoted practitioner, Dennis
has given us a simple but rich gift for improving our
practice of the spiritual discipline of prayer."
— Hayward Armstrong, Ph.D. Director of Master of Christian
Studies, School of Theology and Missions, Union University

"My friend and brother in Christ Dennis Davidson has
written a useful resource on prayer that provides
instruction and encouragement not only for those who
are new to prayer but also for those seasoned in
conversation with God. He draws together words of

insight about the Biblical nature of prayer and couples it with practical helps for the journey of prayer. Davidson's words come not only from research but also from his own personal time with the Lord. His prayers flow from a heart that is intimate with Christ, making prayers an ongoing conversation rather than a daily event."
— Rev. Dave Thomas, Buffat Heights Baptist Church

"Dr. Dennis Davidson has provided a helpful book for disciplined prayer guided by Biblical revelation. *Without Ceasing* delves deep into the dynamics of prayer as an intentional labor of devotion that must be cultivated according to holy design."

"Beyond the expected church jargon and well-known verses is the sharp focus on the act of hearing. Prayer is often misunderstood as monologue when the reality is dialogue. Rather than passively listening, Davidson has accented prayer as active listening that is front-loaded into the conversation. In fact, the believer prepares for prayer, striving to hear the Word before endeavoring to apply the Word. When prayer is embraced as a life-long task, the desired results shift from any personal benefit to the eternal blessings. As such, Davidson points readers to the unity and harmony of a life bathed in prayer, at peace in the presence of God and at work in the will of God."

"*Without Ceasing* is Christ-centered and free from tangents into psychological clichés, cultural cul-de-sacs, or self-help bargains. Instead, prayer is presented as a human response to the divine grace which transforms and redeems. A Christian cannot remain silent in testimony prayer, and this book guides the conversation."
— Daniel E. Hatfield, Ph.D.

Without Ceasing

Without Ceasing

by Dennis Davidson, D. Min.

Publishing
Angel
Climbing

WITHOUT CEASING
Written by Dennis Davidson, D. Min.

Edited by Lisa Soland

Text copyright © 2019 Dr. Dennis Davidson

CAUTION: All rights reserved. No part of this publication may be reproduced, stored in a retrieval system, or transmitted in any form or by any means electronic, mechanical, photocopy, recording, or other, except for brief quotations in written reviews, without the prior written permission of the publisher.

Scripture quotations taken from the New American Standard Bible® (NASB), Copyright © 1960, 1962, 1963, 1968, 1971, 1972, 1973, 1975, 1977, 1995 by The Lockman Foundation
Used by permission. www.Lockman.org

Published in 2019 by
Climbing Angel Publishing
PO Box 32381
Knoxville, Tennessee 37930 http://www.ClimbingAngel.com

First Edition May 2019
Printed in the United States of America
Cover & Author Photograph by Stefan Holt
    Cover model, Pete Wright
Cover design by PrintEdge, Knoxville
Interior design by Climbing Angel Publishing

ISBN: 978-1-64370-033-5

This book is dedicated to my parents
who lived a life of unceasing prayer
and allowed me to behold a God
who graciously acts on behalf
of His people.

Contents

Foreword xv
Introduction xvii

LIVING IN GOD'S PRESENCE
1. The Surrender of Prayer 1
2. The Abiding of Prayer 9
3. The Spirit in Prayer 15

HOW TO HEAR GOD
4. Getting Alone with God 23
5. Listening to God's Voice 29
6. Consistency with God 35
7. The Prayer Notebook & Journaling 41

ELEMENTS OF PRAYER (part 1)
8. Adoration 51
9. Confession 57

ELEMENTS OF PRAYER (part 2)
10. Thanksgiving 65
11. Intercession 71
12. Petition 77

REACHING HEAVEN THROUGH PRAYER
13. Praying in Jesus' Name 85
14. Praying in Faith 91
15. Asking and Receiving 99
16. Unanswered Prayers 103

17. Conditions for Answered Prayer   109

A PRAYER WARRIOR'S ARMOR (part 1)
18. Spiritual Armor   125
19. The Belt of Truth   129
20. The Breastplate of Righteousness   135
21. The Shoes of Peace   141

A PRAYER WARRIOR'S ARMOR (part 2)
22. The Shield of Faith   151
23. The Helmet of Salvation   157
24. The Sword of the Spirit   163

SPIRITUAL WARFARE
25. Spiritual Strongholds   171
26. The Ultimate Spiritual Task   181
27. Praying the Promises   187

BEING UNITED IN PRAYER
28. Unity in Prayer   195
29. Agreement in Prayer   201
30. A House of Prayer   207

Conclusion   213
Notes   215

Foreword

All testimonies are not the same. A reporter can share what he has been told. A philosopher can communicate what he thinks. However, a witness can express what he knows by experience.

Dennis Davidson is a witness about prayer. When he writes about prayer he is sharing personal testimony to what he has experienced to be true in his own life. The author of this book knows prayer because he knows personally and intimately the One to whom he is praying. On numerous occasions, my spirit has been deeply impacted by listening to Dennis lead in prayer. When he prays, Dennis is talking to his Father who he knows and loves.

Dennis has written the book you now hold in the same way he prays—as a personal witness. *Without Ceasing* is the testimony of a devoted follower of Jesus who wants others to join him on the journey of knowing and experiencing the Lord through the disciplines of prayer. Because effective prayer is a discipline, Dennis has structured his witness about prayer in the step by step process of a journey.

He begins with insights on how to prepare your heart to encounter God and then moves with Bible saturated guidance on how to practice effective prayer, how to battle against our adversary in prayer, and then how to unite with other believers in prayer. Dennis' insights on the spiritual disciplines of keeping a prayer notebook and on journaling are worth the price of the entire book. The implementation of the principles and practices he shares in this volume is priceless.

I am so personally grateful for the impact of Dennis on my own life through his prayers. I am thrilled to know that you are about to spend some time with this witness, who when it comes to the subject of prayer, knows what he is talking about, and intimately knows the One of whom he is talking.

Sam Polson
Lead Pastor, West Park Baptist Church
Knoxville, Tennessee
April 2019

Introduction

Prayer is vital for the Christian and for the Church. Prayer is also difficult, demanding, and constantly waylaid by the Christian's and the church's ancient foe. The high cost of prayer in terms of surrender of life, commitment of time, and the sacrifice of spiritual and physical energies often cause even the best of Christians to reallocate prayer to secondary importance. This lack of praying might be understandable and possibly acceptable if the cost of prayerlessness were not so eternally high.

The believer's life and all Christian endeavors are dependent for their success to a large extent on prayer. Christians may live and labor faithfully and it is all for naught without God's involvement, and God's involvement is secured only by prayer (James 4:2-3; John 15:7). Prayer secures the blessings of God on every area of life and ministry of the church. Although it cannot take the place of other ministries, without prayer other ministries are doomed to failure. God, therefore, commands believers to pray without ceasing (I Thessalonians 5:17; Ephesians 6:18).

Despite certain knowledge of the vital necessity of prayer, it will not naturally occur in the life of a Christian nor in the life of a church. Prayer is an *unseen* work or ministry. Because of this, it is often sacrificed for more *seen* needs. Even when prayer becomes a disciplined and vital part of the life of a Christian and a church, it can become somewhat rote and ritualistic even from sincere prayers. This means of developing a relationship of intimacy with Jesus Christ and maturity as a believer is thus in constant danger of eroding away.

Prayer can be boring, ritualistic, and repetitious instead of fresh, alive, and invigorating. The busy-ness of a twenty-first century Christian's daily life and a church's full, demanding, and rushed program exert incessant subtle influences that push prayer off to the side. Because fervent prayer is in constant danger of deterioration, and being persuaded of its vital importance, the development and implementation of a method for strengthening the Christian's personal and the church's corporate prayer life and ministry, is necessary.

Dear believer, let us, therefore, determine anew to enter into the presence of our Lord Jesus and develop the intimacy of relationship that will carry us through the barriers to prayer as well as the difficulties of life. Once again surrender yourself afresh and continue your journey into prayer.

Without Ceasing is a study of discipleship through prayer, by oneself or in a group setting. This book is designed to assist in the development of an intimate, personal relationship with God by learning how to enter into His presence, recognize His voice, and respond to His will. God desires to commune and to communicate with His people concerning their daily situations and needs so that He might make their joy full (John 15:11; 1 John 1:4). Prayer is vital to establish, continue and deepen this relationship.

As you work your way through *Without Ceasing*, you will learn how to walk with God, how to have a meaningful prayer life with God, and how to use prayer to advance the Kingdom of God.

To assist small group study, the book has been divided into nine sections which may be assigned week by week or chapter by individual chapter. Begin each chapter by reading the "key verse" and asking God to open up His Word and make it real and alive. Then read the verse again out loud and begin the study.

As you go through your prayer journey these next few weeks, my prayer is that a renewal and revitalization of not only your prayer life but your life in Christ will occur.

Dennis Davidson
Knoxville, Tennessee
April 2019

Living in God's Presence

1

THE SURRENDER OF PRAYER

*"Search me, O God, and know my heart; try me
and know my anxious thoughts.
And see if there be any hurtful way in me, and
lead me in the everlasting way."
(Psalm 139:23-24)*

There comes a time in a growing Christian's life when one longs for a fuller, more intimate relationship with the Creator. The Psalmist expressed this desire in Psalm 42:1:

> As the deer pants for the water brooks, so my soul pants for You, O God. My soul thirsts for God, for the Living God; When shall I come and appear before God?

When the believer so yearns for intimacy and the presence of God, what should he do? Psalm 139 contains instructions for those who long to draw nearer to God and enter into His presence.

1 O Lord, you have searched me and known me!

You know when I sit down and when I rise up; you discern my thoughts from afar.

You search out my path and my lying down and are acquainted with all my ways.

Even before a word is on my tongue, behold, O Lord, you know it altogether.

You hem me in, behind and before, and lay your hand upon me.

Such knowledge is too wonderful for me; it is high; I cannot attain it.

Where shall I go from your Spirit? Or where shall I flee from your presence?

If I ascend to heaven, you are there! If I make my bed in Sheol, you are there!

If I take the wings of the morning and dwell in the uttermost parts of the sea,

even there your hand shall lead me, and your right hand shall hold me.

If I say, "Surely the darkness shall cover me, and the light about me be night,"

even the darkness is not dark to you; the night is bright as the day,

for darkness is as light with you.

For you formed my inward parts; you knitted me together in my mother's womb.

I praise you, for I am fearfully and wonderfully made.

Wonderful are your works; my soul knows it very well.

My frame was not hidden from you, when I was being made in secret, intricately woven in the depths of the earth. Your eyes saw my unformed substance;

in your book were written, every one of them,

> the days that were formed for me, when as yet there was none of them.
> How precious to me are your thoughts, O God! How vast is the sum of them!
> If I would count them, they are more than the sand. I awake, and I am still with you.
> Oh that you would slay the wicked, O God! O men of blood, depart from me!
> They speak against you with malicious intent; your enemies take your name in vain.
> Do I not hate those who hate you, O Lord? And do I not loathe those who rise up against you?
> I hate them with complete hatred; I count them my enemies.
> 23 Search me, O God, and know my heart! Try me and know my thoughts!
> 24 And see if there be any grievous way in me, and lead me in the way everlasting!
> (Psalm 139)

The Psalmist has looked at God's incredible knowledge, presence, and power. He shudders at the depths God has built into human beings. He realizes that he is not capable of searching out the depths of himself in a way that even approaches adequacy. Yet he longs to know himself in order to come to a fuller understanding of himself so that he might walk with God in an even closer fellowship and greater favor. Thus he opens himself up to God's search.

Verse 23 reads, "Search me, O God, and know my heart; Try me and know my anxious thoughts." From acknowledging that this searching and trying is what God does in verse 1 of Psalm 139, David changes it to a petition and asks God to do it, to search him, in verse 23. David has seen the danger that stalks men and prays that God not let him be self-deluded but lay bare the true state of his soul. David desires God to search out inner enemies with the same diligence as he stood against external enemies on the battlefield. He never wants to be at odds with God but wants the closest communion possible, so he asks God to explore the secret places, the recesses of his own heart, mind, and soul.

David wishes to have God reveal his heart. The plea is to know himself and all his sin and inclinations to sin so that he might be delivered from them. He is thoroughly honest in seeking divine help and is ready for the humbling experience of more honestly seeing himself from God's perspective.

King David asks God to try him and reveal his anxious thoughts. Only a true man of God asks to be put into the crucible of God's innermost revealing. The probing, the proving, and the provoking will be painful and disgustingly revealing, but the end result is greater closeness and empowering of the Holy Spirit. The opportunity will be provided for David to deal in serious repentance with what has been revealed. He will have his faith purified like gold and he will find the peace that only the righteous discipline of the Lord brings.

A true disciple will pray this prayer, but we must be aware of the cost. Yet, once you have been so tested, you become dependable to God and man. It is a test that removes hypocrisy.

> "And see if there be any hurtful way in me, And
> lead me in the everlasting way."
> (Psalm 139:24)

When we love someone we do not shrink from opening up our innermost self to them because we know that the loved one only wants to help. So David makes a matter of anxiety, a matter of prayer to his beloved God.

He desires the all-seeing eye, the all-penetrating One, to open up the chambers of the heart, mind, and soul and reveal attitudes, desires, and characteristics that might pain, hurt, or grieve God. It may be painful to have sin revealed and removed, but it cleanses and heals and leads to health and faithfulness.

This cleansing is the way to personal revival which is revealed in the words "and lead me in the everlasting way." Revival begins only when God's people recognize their sin and receive cleansing from their self-will and pride. Once we are cleansed and pure, God can lead us in the everlasting way.

The everlasting way is the way of righteousness that leads to heaven. Yes, it may be the way of the furnace where the impurities of life are removed but it is the way of faith and godliness. It is the way of the footsteps of Jesus.

To understand the depths of God's love and the completeness of His redemption of us, we must understand the depth of God's knowledge of us. We should be like the little girl who told her mom of the new song she learned in Sunday school, "Jesus knows me this I love." The mother corrected her saying, "Jesus loves me this I know" but either statement should be true.

Sin separates us from God (Isaiah 59:1-2):

> Behold, the Lord's hand is not so short
> That it cannot save;
> Nor is His ear so dull
> That it cannot hear.
> But your iniquities have made a separation
> between you and your God,

> And your sins have hidden His face from you so that He does not hear.

We cannot hide ourselves or our sin from God. Why do we desire to hide who we really are from ourselves? For in the revealing of what we truly are comes with it the possibility of cleansing and sanctification.

Two couples vacationing in England were driving along the shore of a large body of water. As they were discussing whether it was the English Channel or the Falmouth Estuary, they saw two women walking along the sidewalk.

"John, pull over there and I'll ask those ladies if this is the English Channel," said Max. He pulled over, rolled down the window and said to one of the women, "Excuse me, ma'am, is that the English Channel?" She glanced over her shoulder and said, "Well, that's part of it."

That woman's answer also applies to people. Like the English Channel, a large part of who we are lies unseen by others and even ourselves. When we get searched, tried, cleansed, and corrected we can walk in the everlasting way and lead others to greater self-disclosure.

Are you tired of hurting your spouse, your loved ones, or yourself? Do you want God to refine out those hurtful ways? Will you ask Him to search you and will you allow Him to cleanse your life? Will you make a matter-of-fact a matter of prayer? Are you ready to say goodbye to self-delusion and hello to God's everlasting reality?

PERSONAL APPLICATION

1) When you pray a "search me" prayer, you invite God to shine the light of His holiness into the inner recesses of your soul and expose whatever is there. Have you grown sufficiently in your spiritual maturity?

2) Do you trust God enough that you are willing to pray such a prayer? Why or why not?

3) Read Psalm 139 again. Then admit to God you are not what you know He would have you be. Quiet yourself before God and ask Him to search you. Listen for His still, small voice. Now write down thoughts as the Holy Spirit reveals them to you.

4) Over what areas of your life do you sense His conviction? What sins do you need to confess and confront? List the areas of your life that need improvement. Be yielded, sensitive, and responsive to God's leading. Commit yourself to deal with each revealed area of needed growth. (Other Scripture for contemplation: Matthew 12:36-37, Proverb 4:23)

5) Look not only at the obvious concerns but also those more easily hidden. Example: have you sacrificed

someone's feelings in order to build your own self-image? Have you compromised an opportunity to love in order to stay safe? Look at your relationships and your attitude toward others also.

6) What "anxious thoughts" or "hurtful ways" did God reveal to you?

7) Now write your plan of action to correct and improve those areas of need.

2

THE ABIDING OF PRAYER

*"If you abide in Me and My words abide in you,
ask whatever you wish,
and it will be done for you."*
(John 15:7)

To live in the presence of God is to abide in God's Word. You cannot abide in Jesus without abiding in His Word. If you abide in Jesus by conforming your life to His Word, you abide in prayer or in the continuous constant communication of a living relationship.

Apparently, not all believers who are indwelt by the Holy Spirit at their point of belief in Jesus, continue to abide in Him, though they have received the power to do so. What does abide mean anyway? Abide in the Greek (μείνητε) is in the aorist or punctiliar past tense, indicating a permanent abiding. The word is also translated—remain, dwell, or live. It is a favorite word of John, used forty times in His Gospel, and when used in connection with Jesus the word indicates a complete dependence upon Him.

The power for abiding in Christ comes from Christ, but grace can be rejected. So, the responsibility for receiving this grace needed for abiding is placed with man. To remain in communion with Christ is to live by faith in Him, for faith is the means of receiving grace. It is only by abiding or living in Christ that the believer develops, grows, and bears spiritual fruit. Apart from Christ, the believer can do nothing of eternal worth or value.

> I am the vine, you are the branches; he who
> abides in Me and I in him, he bears much fruit,
> for apart from Me you can do nothing.
> (John 15:5)

To abide is to open our heart so that He may fill it with His Spirit, grace, and power. It also means to turn away from every influence that would draw us from Jesus or cause us to substitute anything for our relationship with Him.

The indication is given that if one is abiding in Christ, then Jesus' Words are abiding in him. How we live in Christ is by receiving Christ's Words or utterances into our heart and mind and then by daily following or obeying them. Here, "Words" or "utterances" (rēmata) is plural. Through a permanent embracing of Christ and His precepts and principles, a spiritual union is formed. By continuing in His Word that relationship bond is strengthened. The abiding by faith in Christ is demonstrated by giving permanent residence to His Word. This living out of the Word by faith causes and strengthens one's union with Christ, and, blessing upon blessings, through this union, Christ's life and power become available to the believer. When we cherish His Word by applying His Words, His presence and power live in and through us.

The astounding promise given to those who live in Christ and in His Word is that whatever they may ask will be done for them. The reason this promise is so true is that those who are living in the complete control of Christ's words will ask for nothing contrary to God's will. They ask in the spirit of "not my will, but Yours be done" (Luke 22:42). A person asking out of such a union of relation between himself and God will receive what he asks.

"Ask" is in the imperative, meaning we must ask. When we walk in harmony with Christ, He commands us to ask so that we might receive. There are no limits placed on our asking because there is no limit to what He can give. The only limit is the faith of the one given the authority and responsibility to ask. Faith in Jesus, demonstrated by receiving and living out His Word, establishes a relationship through which Christ's life and power are made available to the believer. This glorious promise is even a more glorious reality for those who live in the inspiration and guidance of His Word.

PERSONAL APPLICATION

1) Read John 15:1-17. Is your life one of complete surrender to Jesus? If not, what areas do you still need to surrender?

2) Do you have a growing relationship because you are vitally connected to Him in your faith, love, and obedience? In what ways do you exercise and draw upon this relationship?

3) Do you read, meditate, study, memorize, and above all abide in or obey His Word? Which area(s) need improvement? How do you plan on improving?

4) What fruit are you bearing in your Christian life? If you feel you are bearing little fruit is it because there is little prayer?

5) In Jesus Christ can be found all that we will ever need. Christ places at the disposal of those who live in Him, all the treasures of heaven if we will only search them out in His Word and ask for them. What are some things lacking with your spiritual life/relationship with Christ?

6) How do you plan to improve upon these things that are lacking? How can you apply Christ's promises in these areas?

7) Are you growing in love, faith, and obedience to Christ? If not, why? Or, if so, how?

3

THE SPIRIT IN PRAYER
"...not I but Christ"

I have been crucified with Christ; and it is no longer I who live, but Christ lives in me; and the life which I now live in the flesh I live by faith in the Son of God, who loved me, and delivered Himself up for me."
(Galatians 2:20)

Prayer must be to the Father through the Son and by the Holy Spirit.

...for through Him we both have our access in one Spirit to the Father. (Ephesians 2:18)

The Spirit can pray in a believer *only* when the believer lives in the Spirit and is filled with the Spirit. Only as the believer dies to self and lives in complete surrender to Jesus can one live in and be filled with the Holy Spirit. God gives His Spirit to be the divine power that prays in the believer's heart to draw him upward to heaven. God is Spirit and nothing but spiritual life given by the indwelling Spirit within man can have communion with Him. This living fellowship will certainly manifest itself by praying in the Spirit.

To pray in the Spirit is to pray in the power of the resurrected Christ. To live or pray in the power of the resurrected Christ you must first die to self, to the natural man, to the person that you were before you encountered Jesus Christ. You die to self by appropriating or taking hold of the power of the cross. You do this by placing yourself, your desires, aspirations, and dreams on the cross with Christ and dying to them. Then by the power of Christ living within, you take up His desires, aspirations, and dreams for your life. Only after you have died to self and become alive to God by faith will you be able to yield yourself to the Spirit's movement within you.

The Holy Spirit is the indwelling presence of Christ in every believer. He is indispensable to the prayer life of each Christian. Effective prayer is spiritual prayer. It is prayer that is led by the Holy Spirit. The Holy Spirit gives believers spiritual thoughts, and words, and reveals the thoughts of God.

> Now we have received, not the spirit of the world, but the Spirit who is from God, so that we may know the things freely given to us by God, which things we also speak, not in words taught by human wisdom, but in those taught by the Spirit, combining spiritual thoughts with spiritual words. (1 Corinthians 2:12-13)

The believer is instructed to pray at all times in the Spirit.

> With all prayer and petition pray at all times in the Spirit, and with this in view, be on the alert

> with all perseverance and petition for all the saints, (Ephesians 6:18)

Every prayer is to proceed from the mind of the Spirit. A disciple should develop a prayer life where the Holy Spirit is in control. Being filled with the Spirit means being entirely yielded to the Holy Spirit, and being influenced and guided by Him alone. The Holy Spirit can only pray through the believer *when* the believer lives a life of total surrender to God by the power of the cross and resurrection of Jesus.

Prayer is the breathing of the Spirit within the believer.[1] Effective prevailing prayer depends on the indwelling of the Spirit.[2] In *How to Pray*, R. A. Torrey states, "It is the prayer that God the Holy Spirit inspires that God the Father answers."[3] In faith, the believer should cast himself in complete dependency upon the Holy Spirit to guide his utterances. The Spirit knows the Word and will of God, and He will enliven faith within the believer to lay hold of the promises of God.

> "Praying men are the only ones in whom the Holy Spirit dwells, because the Holy Spirit and prayer go hand in hand."
> (E. M. Bounds, *The Weapon of Prayer*)[4]

To be "in the Spirit" is to be surrounded by His presence and power. This transforms the motivation and attitude of the Christian before, during, and after praying. By dependence on the Spirit and in cooperation with Him, even when the believer does not have the right words or any words to express his thoughts, the Holy Spirit expresses the deep needs of the heart to the Father (Romans 8:26-27).

In the same way the Spirit also helps our weakness; for we do not know how to pray as we should, but the Spirit Himself intercedes for us with groanings too deep for words; and He who searches the hearts knows what the mind of the Spirit is, because He intercedes for the saints according to the will of God.

The Spirit of the indwelling Christ reveals the Son and the Father and brings about the fullest trust and deepest fellowship possible this side of heaven.

PERSONAL APPLICATION

1) Read Galatians 2:20 again. Have you ever taken hold of the power of the cross to die to your old self? If not, do so now. Think of areas of sinfulness, temptation, and failure and give them to Christ. Then apply the power of the cross and die to them.

2) Do you sense the Holy Spirit leading you when you spend time in prayer? What have been some spiritual thoughts He has given you? Do you seek the mind of the Spirit while you are praying concerning a matter?

3) Is it difficult to surrender the leadership of your life to the Holy Spirit? Why do you think this is so?

4) Does God hear you if you do not pray in the Spirit? Why do you think your prayers are more effective and more likely to be answered if you pray in the Spirit?

5) Will the Spirit ever speak to you or lead you contrary to the Word of God? If this occurred, what would be influencing you?

How to Hear God

4

GETTING ALONE WITH GOD

*But you, when you pray, go into your inner
room, close your door and pray to your Father
who is in secret, and your Father who sees what
is done in secret will reward you.
(Matthew 6:6)*

This world is a complex, busy, demanding, and overall, a distracting place. It is difficult to maintain God's presence in such an atmosphere, much less encounter it. To find God's presence and hear His still, small voice requires, especially at first, a pulling away. The soul and spirit of every believer needs daily tuning by God *before* one gets caught up and tied into society's agenda, objectives, and activities that can force one away from his walk with God. Elements of this section, "How to Hear God," will assist you in this sacred privilege of seeking God's face and finding His favor. For all who will recognize their need and dependence, the Father sits waiting at the Throne of Grace.

Although the believer will often need to pray with others and with the church united, one should always seek God's face before they seek the face of anyone else. This is certainly the pattern of Jesus' life.

Jesus sought solitude so He could be alone with the Father. He sought out secluded places so that He, sometimes along with His disciples, could pray undisturbed. His chosen sanctuaries were the mountains, the desert, on or by a lake, or in a garden (Matthew 14:15, 23; Mark 6:46; Luke 5:16, 6:12; John 18:2). Even when in crowds, in the solitude of His being, He prayed (Luke 9:18).[5]

> And it happened that while He was praying alone, the disciples were with Him, and He questioned them, saying, "Who do the people say that I am?"

Jesus instructed His disciples in the Model Prayer to go to the Father in secret (Matthew 6:6):

> But you, when you pray, go into your inner room, close your door and pray to your Father who is in secret, and your Father who sees what is done in secret will reward you.

Intimacy with God is developed in private communion. Closing off the outer world makes it easier to enter the inner sanctuary. The shutting out of the tumults of the world assists one entering into the contrition of the heart that recognizes God's presence.[6] This leaving of the sensual, fleshly, and external opens the way to enter into the spiritual and eternal. By entering into the secret closet and shutting the door to the world, one finds the peaceful presence of the indwelling Christ.[7]

The sweetness of this inner sanctum affords the solace and strength to carry on the work of prayer. Time alone with God opens the way for His healing, teaching, and guiding to occur. As undivided attention is given to Him, loneliness is relieved, and repair of the damage and pressure of the world takes place. When God has one's full attention, His thoughts are more clearly heard. During this time of complete surrender to God, one should be open to doing anything in line with the Word of God that He impresses upon the heart. While abiding in His peaceful presence the Lord protects from deception, calls forth into deeper communion, and clearly speaks from His Word.[8] The closed door to the world and an open door to God provide God the stillness needed to speak to man's deepest needs.

PERSONAL APPLICATION

1) Why do you think Jesus sought solitude to pray?

2) Why do you think Jesus took His disciples away for times of extended prayer and relaxation?

3) Do you have a set time and place to meet with God each day? If not, why?

4) What could you do to start a daily time with God, or if you have one, how can you improve it?

5) What are several things you enjoy about your private time with God?

6) Do you encounter distractions in your quiet time with God? List some of these distractions and what you can do to avoid them?

5

LISTENING TO GOD'S VOICE

*"My sheep hear My voice, and I know them,
and they follow Me."*
(John 10:27)

God speaks to men in various ways. His voice may be still and small and heard in the inner spirit, or it may be heard through the wonder of His creation. He also speaks through His people, and can sometimes use the circumstances of life to communicate His message. The clearest, most certain way He communicates to man is by His Word—the Holy Scriptures. Bible meditation and prayer are vitally connected. By the Word, God speaks to the disciple, and through the Word, He quickens the spirit, heart, mind, and soul of the believer.

Prayer is not a monologue but a dialogue. Prayer is not to be a one-sided conversation in which we talk to God and hear nothing from Him. Listening to God's voice gives the assurance that God is dialoguing with the disciple. God's Word prepares the disciple by revealing what the Father's will is and what the Father desires to be asked.[9] As one listens to the Word of God, one's heart, mind, and soul become attuned to God and comes to know His voice. This listening to the Living God through His Word brings one into the presence of God.

> The Lord is near to all who call upon Him,
> To all who call upon Him in truth.
> (Psalm 145:18)

In His presence, the living voice of God enters and brings wisdom, strength, and blessing; which will awaken the listener's faith so that he might reach out and find God's hand, feel His heart, and speak into His ear.

> "If you abide in Me, and My words abide in you, ask whatever you wish and it shall be done for you." (John 15:7)

Having God's Word constantly in the believer's life reproduces the life and will of Jesus within the disciple. This abiding in God's Word reproduces Jesus' character, disposition, and conduct until the listener's life is completely influenced by Christ. As the Word changes the surrendered listener, he then becomes not only an influence for Christ but on Christ. The disciple's Holy Spirit inspired prayer is received and God acts because of it. As the words of God abide in the believer, the Lordship of Christ exerts its influence. The disciple not only prays in the Spirit according to the will of God but also lives in his physical body according to the will of God. When the believer follows God or lives what God says because he has heard God in his inner being, God will hear and do whatever His obedient child asks resulting in the glorification of the Father.

> This is the confidence which we have before Him, that, if we ask anything according to His will, He hears us. And if we know that He hears us in whatever we ask, we know that we have the requests which we have asked from Him. (1 John 5:14-15).

The more earnestly one enters into the Lord's Word the more certain one prays according to God's will and the more certain the response of heaven.[10]

PERSONAL APPLICATION

1) How one-sided are your conversations with God? Are you more interested in God hearing you or in you hearing God?

2) How are you sure that you are as interested in hearing God as you are in Him hearing you?

3) Most relationship problems occur because either one or both parties are poor listeners. How would you rate your listening to God? How can you improve?

4) Have you ever prayed the Word back to God? Listening to what God says to you through His Word will give you guidance in what He would have you pray. Isaiah 30:21 says, "Your ears will hear a voice behind you saying, 'This is the way, walk in it.'"

5) Describe an occurrence when God fulfilled His Word to you in this way. How did you know it was God? Who spoke or acted?

6

CONSISTENCY WITH GOD

"In the morning, while it was still dark, Jesus got up, left, and went away to a secluded place and was praying there."
(Mark 1:35)

An effective prayer life requires discipline and commitment. Prayer is hard work. If this were not the case, more people would pray more often for longer periods of time. Without a systematically ordered prayer life, the effort may seem too difficult.

Though the believer is to pray *without ceasing* and in any place, it is best to have a specific time and place to meet with God. This place should be quiet, comfortable and well lit. Over time, whenever the believer sits or kneels in that place, he will begin to sense the presence of God waiting for him. The place becomes a sanctuary where one is alone with God.

The best time for prayer seems to be in the early morning when one is refreshed and not yet caught up in daily activities. Scripture encourages it,[11] and it appears to have been the pattern of Jesus' life.[12] Establishing a morning

"Armor of God" by Francesco Pussumato
permission from dreamstime.com

routine may help prepare the disciple. For example, when a believer begins to wake up, he should get up and get moving. Perhaps starting the day with light exercise, a shower, and maybe even a cup of coffee can help prepare a disciple who has set aside this time as a definite priority with a definite purpose. The child of God is getting ready to meet with God for the purpose of hearing Him speak and to bring his thoughts before Him. Those who intend to deepen and expand their relationship with Jesus will be serious about regularly meeting with Him and will prepare themselves to do so!

Now that the disciple has situated himself, he needs a plan for his daily appointment with God. Once he is ready, if he has not done so already, he will want to put on each piece of the spiritual armor in prayer.

> Put on the full armor of God, so that you will be able to stand firm against the schemes of the devil. For our struggle is not against flesh and blood, but against the rulers, against the powers, against the world forces of this darkness, against the spiritual forces of wickedness in the heavenly places. Therefore, take up the full armor of God, so that you will be able to resist in the evil day, and having done everything, to stand firm. Stand firm therefore, having girded your loins with truth, and having put on the breastplate of righteousness, and having shod your feet with the preparation of the gospel of peace; in addition to all, taking up the shield of faith with which you will be able to extinguish all the flaming arrows of the evil one. And take the helmet of salvation, and the sword of the Spirit, which is the word of God. With all prayer and

> petition pray at all times in the Spirit, and with this in view, be on the alert with all perseverance and petition for all the saints... (Ephesians 6:11-18)

After he has asked God to open his eyes (Psalm 119:18) and ears (Isaiah 50:4), he should begin reading the Word of God.

The disciple should read the Bible in a systematic manner, paragraph by paragraph, in order to understand verses in their context. If time is limited and there is little time for prayer, let it be spent by God speaking to the disciple through His Word. "It is more important that God speak to the individual than the individual speak to God."[13] The length of the passage should be determined by time constraints and the needs of the believer. The main concern is to hear God speak to the heart and mind through His Word so that one becomes attuned to His voice and will.

While the disciple reads, he should be aware of Scriptures that are promises to be claimed for someone on his prayer list. There will also be verses that the Holy Spirit impresses upon the heart that will need to be memorized or studied further. Continue the prayer time by going through the various forms or types of prayer. First, "Praise God for the unspeakable love which invites you to come to Him and converse freely with Him."[14] Many find a hymnbook a good tool for their praise and worship times.

Next, ask God to reveal any sin that is hindering the believer's life and relationship with his Father. Thank God for His recent benefits and for the assurance that He will be there every moment and in every situation of the day. Then enter into a time of intercession and petition. These forms of prayer will be discussed further in Sections three and four.

PERSONAL APPLICATION

1) Do you have consistent daily time with God? If so, what time and place does it occur?

2) Has it been difficult to discipline yourself to meet with God daily?

3) What successes have been involved in establishing this priority? What have been some of the challenges?

4) If you don't have a consistent daily time with God, take a moment now and pray that God reveal to you the value of meeting with Him consistently? Ask God to guide you with this new beginning.

5) If you already have an established prayer time, ask God how He would like to change it or improve upon it.

7

THE PRAYER NOTEBOOK & JOURNALING

*I will stand on my guard post
And station myself on the rampart;
And I will keep watch to see what He will speak to me,
And how I may reply when I am reproved.
Then the Lord answered me and said,
"Record the vision
And inscribe it on tablets,
That the one who reads it may run.
"For the vision is yet for the appointed time;
It hastens toward the goal and it will not fail.
Though it tarries, wait for it;
For it will certainly come, it will not delay.*
(Habakkuk 2:1-3)

Developing a notebook for prayers, Scriptures, and guidance can be a valuable tool in becoming more consistent in your quiet time with the Lord. The items that will form the notebook need some initial organization. A small loose-leaf notebook, 8 1/2" x 5" is easier to handle (of course this system may be set up as a computer table). Center at the top of the page, the heading of the designated person or subject matter to be prayed for. Under this prayer topic heading, place four subheading columns. Write the words: Date, Prayer Concern, Promise or appropriate Scripture verse, and in the last column, write God's Answer and Date. This notebook will grow as the disciple's prayer life grows so a loose-leaf notebook is advisable.

Within the prayer notebook, there needs to be a system for praying for different groups or topics on different days or the prayer list can become overwhelming. Name the first divider, "Daily." The daily prayer list should include at least a page for each immediate family member. Naturally, it will have requests or promises God impresses on the prayer's heart during daily devotions. Also include the request that family members surrender to the Lordship of Jesus Christ by daily dying to self by the power of the cross, and that they live in the power of the resurrection. Have a page for the person's pastor and church staff members. Start another page for temporary concerns like sick friends, harmful or special circumstances, or urgent concerns. Also, have a page for personal items which the disciple daily lifts up for themselves.

Next, after the daily prayer section, start a weekly prayer section or lists which will be broken down into different categories for each day of the week. An example would be to pray by name for specific missionaries and lost people on Monday. Tuesday could be devoted to prayer for saints such as deacons, Sunday school teachers, choir and other local church concerns. Wednesday could be the day the individual prays for themselves; for personal disciplines, relationships, attitudes, and a time of confessing who they are in Christ.[15] The prayer book might also contain another division for personal guidance. Where life purpose verses could be listed along with other daily, weekly, monthly, or life goals.[16] Make Thursday a special day of praise and thanksgiving that ends in prayer for extended family and close friends. Friday pray for the President, the Congress, the Senate, and the judiciary system. Include state and local government officials, schools, teachers, and community law officers. Saturday pray for matters worthy of attention like elections, the abortion rampage, and revival in the church. Sunday pray for pastors the Lord is using in special ways, churches, colleges, and seminaries for which you have a burden or interest. Add more subjects and people as the Lord reveals them to you.

A personal prayer journal should be added as another valuable tool for an effective prayer life. "Make a habit to record in it what God says to you."[17] The one who is praying should write down "meaningful Scriptures that are relevant to your life situation."[18] The disciple may want to go back and look through his journal during times of decision, crisis, or despondency.

Many of God's saints have found great help and spiritual blessing through the discipline of keeping a spiritual journal. Just as it takes tools like a hammer and saw to build a sturdy structure, we need good tools to help us more effectively pray and grow spiritually. Journaling is one of those simple, practical, basic tools we need to add to our prayer life.

It is rare to notice changes in your life. One reason we don't see how we are changing is because most of us live unexamined lives. "We repeat the same errors day after day. We don't learn much from the decisions we make, whether they are good or bad. We don't know why we're here or where we're going. One of the benefits of journaling is to force us to examine our lives."[19]

Many Christians feel they have no testimony. That, of course, is not true. They simply do not recall how God has worked in their lives. They forget the overwhelming joy of the arrival of their first born, how God watched over them in specific ways at specific times, or God's presence in times of bereavement or tragedy. Over time journals may record the important lessons, blessings, and spiritual growth "that might otherwise go unnoticed and/or unmeasured. Also, journals provide records of God's answers to prayers and other good gifts received from the Father."[20]

Journaling is an important step in slowing down to pray. It helps focus our thoughts on our life. Journaling helps us get in touch with and express our feelings. It can be used to express events, feelings, and anticipations as you would to a good friend. If used as a spiritual tool it helps free the Spirit to operate that we might walk and talk with Christ as we should.

The most difficult step in any new discipline is often the first step, so go buy yourself a spiral notebook. Taking time to write a journal entry the very first time, is a hurdle that keeps many Christians from developing this tool. Plan to write in your journal every day but restrict yourself to a page, or two, if it's a small notebook. At the beginning or conclusion of each day, take time to open the notebook to the next blank sheet of paper, date it and write. Write a paragraph or two recounting the day's or yesterday's events. Sum up the day and record any lessons learned.

"Write whatever you want—perhaps a little description of the people you interacted with, your appointments, calls, decisions, thoughts, feelings, high points, low points, frustrations, what you remember from your Bible reading, what you were going to do and didn't."[21] This exercise can be a tremendous step forward in spiritual development.

Now, ask God to open your eyes and ears.

> Open my eyes, that I may behold
> Wonderful things from Your law.
> (Psalm 119:18)

Before journaling read a paragraph or a chapter or two in the Bible. Write down in your journal any thoughts or impressions God gives you.

After you have reacted with God's Word, you may want to write out a prayer to God. By this time you have slowed down enough that you may be able to hear God's "gentle whisper."

> So He said, "Go forth and stand on the mountain before the Lord." And behold, the Lord was passing by! And a great and strong wind was rending the mountains and breaking in pieces the rocks before the Lord; but the Lord was not in the wind. And after the wind an earthquake, but the Lord was not in the earthquake. After the earthquake a fire, but the Lord was not in the fire; and after the fire a sound of a gentle blowing. (1 Kings 19:11-12)

In this solitude of unhurried communing of God's Spirit with our spirit, listen and write anything you hear God impressing upon your heart and mind. You may want to spend this portion of your quiet time on your knees waiting in humble respect and anticipation. Strength comes out of solitude. Decisions that change your life usually come out of these *holy of holies* times.

After you have jotted down your thoughts on your Bible portion, open your prayer notebook. First, lift up your daily prayers, and then go to your weekly prayers and pray about these items.

Enjoy journaling. This practice is not intended to be an ordeal, but an aid to your spiritual life and growth. Journaling is a basic tool that enables you to realize what is going on in your life, to enjoy God's presence more, to hear and reflect on what He is saying to you through His Word, through life, and through His Holy Spirit.

PERSONAL APPLICATION

1) Have you developed a prayer notebook?

2) What is your favorite aspect of your prayer plan?

3) In what ways are you challenged by developing this tool?

4) Have you ever kept a journal?

5) How have these tools assisted you in your spiritual journey?

Elements of Prayer
(part 1)

8

ADORATION

"Pray, then, in his way:
'Our Father who is in heaven,
Hallowed be Your name.
'Your kingdom come.
Your will be done,
On earth as it is in heaven.'"
(Matthew 6:9-10)

Since man's relationship with God is multifaceted, so is prayer.[22] The effective prayer life of the praying believer will usually be focused through particular types of prayers. An understanding of these various types will assist in unfolding one's dialogue with the Father, as well as expand the scope and depth of one's relationship with God. Though the definition of these forms varies, there are five elements that should be present in a well-balanced prayer life.

The model prayer that Jesus used to teach His disciples how to pray, begins and ends with adoration.

Pray, then, in this way:
'Our Father who is in heaven,

Hallowed be Your name.
'Your kingdom come.
Your will be done,
On earth as it is in heaven.

'Give us this day our daily bread.
'And forgive us our debts, as we also have forgiven our debtors.
'And do not lead us into temptation, but deliver us from evil. For Yours is the kingdom and the power and the glory forever. Amen.'
(Matthew 6:9-13)

Jesus' teaching implies that glorifying God is the leading and major purpose of prayer. The one praying should praise God because of who He is and for His response to man's requests. Praising God is an act of worship that acknowledges and exalts His character and deeds. Worship is the most appropriate way to enter into the presence of the Most High and Holy Sovereign of the Universe.

Adoration sets the proper tone for prayer. Worship causes us to remember who we are addressing and into whose presence we are seeking entrance. Prayer begins by focusing on God, who He is, and what He does. God must be given the first priority in praying because He is the highest worth and must be given the highest respect.[23] Worship asks nothing from God but is the simple act of becoming absorbed with Him. When one so focuses on God, one finds God's attributes worthy of praise. Studying the attributes or nature of God helps in recognizing God's supreme value, perfection, and excellences.

Yahweh is the Creator, Re-creator, and Sustainer of all. El Shaddai is exalted high above the highest heavens. All other beings and all other things pale to insignificance when compared to Him. The Sovereign Lord is altogether holy, truthful, loving, kind, merciful, just, all-knowing, all-powerful, and all-present. The King of Glory is wise, patient, magnificent, glorious, healing, forgiving, and gracious. The Prince of Peace is attentive, humble, willing to provide, and unchanging. With reverence and awe, believers bow down before the Almighty and adore the splendor of His majesty and holiness. Since the Everlasting Father is respected and loved above all others, He should receive the highest acclaim, honor, and admiration. Let all mankind give glory to the Lamb that was slain!

Prayer should normally begin with praise because the believer seeks entrance into the courts of the Most High where everything that has breath is currently praising the Lord God Almighty. Bowing in awe before the Creator and adoringly acknowledging who He is and what He has done, causes prayer to take its proper focus. Worship purges our thoughts and spirit and softens our heart. When we praise God He inhabits our praises and us. Oh, the wonder of His goodness, love, mercy, and grace!

May we say with David, "My praise is continually of You." And I "will praise You yet more and more."

> By You I have been sustained from my birth;
> You are He who took me from my mother's womb; My praise is continually of You.
> (Psalm 71:6)
>
> But as for me, I will hope continually,
> And will praise You yet more and more.
> (Psalm 71:14)

PERSONAL APPLICATION

1) Which character trait or attribute of God is your favorite? Why?

2) Finish the following sentence as if spoken to the Lord. "I will worship You and praise You because You are..."

3) At least eight compound names are used for God in the Old Testament. Which one of these titles is your favorite? Why?

- The LORD our Righteousness
- The LORD who Sanctifies
- The LORD who is our Peace
- The LORD is Present
- The LORD who Heals
- The LORD who Provides
- The LORD my Banner
- The LORD who is my Shepherd

4) What problems you are currently facing?

5) What character traits or attributes of God address your needs?

6) Some passages that will assist you in your praise are the following:

- Psalm 8
- Psalm 46
- Psalm 148
- Psalm 100
- Psalm 19
- Psalm 47
- Luke 1:46-55
- Psalm 29:3-9
- Psalm 23
- Psalm 95
- Luke 1:68-79

9

CONFESSION

"If we confess our sins, He is faithful and righteous to forgive us our sin and cleanse us from all unrighteousness."
(1 John 1:9)

Seeing God for who He is will give us the clarity to see ourselves for who we are. Entering with praise into God's Holy Presence should bring about conviction of one's sinfulness. Realizing one's shortcomings, failures, and sins before God should cause repentant confession to occur. When Isaiah found himself in God's heavenly presence, he cried out...

"Woe is me, for I am ruined!
Because I am a man of unclean lips,
And I live among a people of unclean lips;
For my eyes have seen the King, the Lord of hosts." (Isaiah 6:5)

God is holy and man lives a sinful existence that falls short of the glory of God. With God's presence, man's condition can be realized. And man's heart, which is in deep contrition because of evil, cries out in sincere resolve to be finished with sin. This is the Holy Spirit's work of conviction.

> And He, when He comes, will convict the world concerning sin and righteousness and judgment; concerning sin, because they do not believe in Me; and concerning righteousness, because I go to the Father and you no longer see Me; and concerning judgment, because the ruler of this world has been judged.
>
> "I have many more things to say to you, but you cannot bear *them* now. But when He, the Spirit of truth, comes, He will guide you into all the truth; for He will not speak on His own initiative, but whatever He hears, He will speak; and He will disclose to you what is to come. He will glorify Me, for He will take of Mine and will disclose *it* to you. All things that the Father has are Mine; therefore I said that He takes of Mine and will disclose *it* to you. (John 16:8-15)

The word confession (ὁμολογια) comes from a compound Greek word that literally means "same-word." Confession is agreeing with God about His judgment of an action or a non-action and about its seriousness.[24] It means to view sin from God's perspective and concur that His way is right.

> How blessed is he whose transgression is forgiven,
> Whose sin is covered!
> How blessed is the man to whom the Lord does not impute iniquity,
> And in whose spirit there is no deceit!

> When I kept silent about my sin, my body wasted away
> Through my groaning all day long.
> For day and night Your hand was heavy upon me;
> My vitality was drained away as with the fever heat of summer. Selah.
>
> I acknowledged my sin to You, And my iniquity I did not hide;
> I said, "I will confess my transgressions to the Lord";
> And You forgave the guilt of my sin. Selah.
> (Psalm 32:1-5)

Sin is anything that displeases God. Confession is agreeing with God that one's sin is sin. Continuous confessing, repenting, and cleansing open the door to a deeper and freer relationship with God. Confession brings a *cleansing of the heart* from an evil conscience so that man can experience a clear and renewed conscience.

> Beloved, if our heart does not condemn us, we have confidence before God; and whatever we ask we receive from Him, because we keep His commandments and do the things that are pleasing in His sight. (1 John 3:21-22)

When sins and sinfulness are repentantly confessed, then the believer's relationship with God is restored so that he experiences the fuller cleansing power of the healing blood of Jesus. Then one's consciousness can be awakened to his wonderful privilege of intimate access and relationship with God.

If we confess our sins, He is faithful and righteous to forgive us our sins and to cleanse us from all unrighteousness.
(1 John 1:9)

My little children, I am writing these things to you so that you may not sin. And if anyone sins, we have an Advocate with the Father, Jesus Christ the righteous...
(1 John 2:1)

PERSONAL APPLICATION

1) Do you encounter God's presence when you pray?

2) Ask God to reveal your sins. What was done that should not have been done?

3) Did you sin with your mind, eyes, lips, stomach, heart, hands, feet...?

4) What was *said* that should not have been said? What was *not said* that should have been said?

5) What was *thought* that should not have been thought? What *should* have been thought about, instead?

6) What has not been done that God expected to be accomplished?

7) Was there a failure to love, to speak, to help, to give, to worship, to be thankful, to forgive, to be reconciled, to be honest...etc?

Elements of Prayer
(part 2)

10

THANKSGIVING

"Be anxious for nothing, but in everything by prayer and supplication with thanksgiving let your requests be made known to God."
(Philippians 4:6)

A heart that has been forgiven, cleansed, and restored spiritually to health and relationship is thankful. Thankfulness is the glad expression and "appreciative acknowledgment of the benefits and blessings God gives."[25] The praise of thanksgiving should always follow answered prayer.

> Bless the Lord, O my soul,
> And all that is within me, bless His holy name.
> Bless the Lord, O my soul,
> And forget none of His benefits;
> Who pardons all your iniquities,
> Who heals all your diseases;
> Who redeems your life from the pit,
> Who crowns you with lovingkindness and compassion...
>
> Who satisfies your years with good things,

> So that your youth is renewed like the eagle.
> Bless the Lord, O my soul,
> And forget none of His benefits...
> (Psalm 103:1-5)

"Thanks should be offered not only for our personal blessings but for all of those wonderful things that we share with others."[26] The praying disciple needs to thank God for what He has done, is doing, and will do.

Being grateful to God declares an acknowledgment to God as the source of every good gift. This attitude is kindled by serious meditation on what God has done for us. Thanksgiving is the grateful remembrance of the love and kindness God has lavished upon the recipient. Thankfulness reminds us of our dependence upon God. Returning thanks for blessings already received increases faith and enables the grateful heart to approach God with new boldness and assurance. When preparing to ask God for new blessings, one "should never forget to return thanks for the blessings already received."[27] The praying disciple should be just as constant in returning thanks as he is in petitioning God for new requests.

If an attitude of thanksgiving permeates prayer, it opens the door for the peace of God which passes all comprehension to guard the heart and mind of the one praying.

> And the peace of God, which surpasses all
> comprehension, will guard your hearts and
> your minds in Christ Jesus. (Philippians 4:7)

Being thankful in prayer causes the believer to be alert in his praying. Colossians 4:2 states, "Devote yourselves to prayer, keeping alert in it with an attitude of thanksgiving..." Giving thanks is the very life of prayer! Paul uses words like "all," "always," and "everything" along with "thanksgiving" to describe a proper prayer attitude.[28] This attitude keeps the praying disciple from developing an attitude of materialism because it acknowledges that God can work His good pleasure, as Romans 8:28 indicates, out of any and all things, whether they appear to be good or bad.[29]

> And we know that God causes all things to work together for good to those who love God, to those who are called according to His purpose. (Romans 8:28)

After we enter into the full, continual presence of the Lord God Almighty, all other forms of prayers will cease, *but* thanksgiving and praise will be the believer's eternal joy. Prayer is a great place to develop an attitude of gratitude! Count your many blessings and thank God for the specific things He has done.

"We thank You, our great God, for the proofs of Your gracious love and wondrous kindness!"

PERSONAL APPLICATION

1) What answer to prayer are you most grateful for right now?

2) For what recent event or circumstance would you like to thank God?

3) Bring to mind at least three people who have done something for you for which you are thankful. What was it they did? Have you shown them gratitude?

4) Bring to mind at least one specific blessing for each of the *type of blessings* listed below:

    - Answered prayers
    - Spiritual blessings
    - Relational blessings
    - Material blessings

5) Offer up thanks to God for each of the specific blessings listed above.

11

INTERCESSION

"Therefore He is able also to save forever those who draw near to God through Him, since He always lives to make intercession for them."
(Hebrews 7:25)

A fourth element of effective praying is *intercession*. Intercession is the offering up of concerns on behalf of the needs and interests of others. When we pray for others, as when we pray for ourselves, we draw near to God to draw down His blessings of grace. We act as an intermediary between God and man. Jesus Christ is the ultimate intercessor and calls Christians to join with Him in this blessed Kingdom privilege.

Scripture says that Jesus lives to make intercession for His people (Hebrew 7:25). Jesus is pleading the Christian's case before His Father and answering any charges against them with the application of His redemptive sacrifice for them.

> Who will bring a charge against God's elect? God is the one who justifies; who is the one who condemns? Christ Jesus is He who died, yes,

rather who was raised, who is at the right hand of God, who also intercedes for us.
(Romans 8:33-34)

Jesus is our ultimate intercessor. It is what He says before the throne of grace on our behalf that makes all the difference.

The grand purpose of intercession is to advance the Kingdom of God on Earth. Because of the burdening and empowering of the Holy Spirit, the intercessor places his requests before God that His will might prevail in specific people and circumstances. Intercessory prayers provide zeal for the Kingdom's enterprises. By intercession comes the empowering for missionary expansion, the conviction of sin, the justice of God, the healing of the sick, the transformation of lives, and the preservation of others—the list goes on and on.

In intercession, we are so moved by compassion, that another's needs become our own. The intercessor acts as Abraham did for the people of Sodom (Genesis 18:23-33) or as Moses did when he stood between God's righteous judgment and the sins of Israel (Exodus 32:1-14). Some intercessors can identify so deeply with those on whose behalf they are praying, that, like Paul, they would be willing to be accursed for the sake of their kinsmen.

> For I could wish that I myself were accursed, separated from Christ for the sake of my brethren, my kinsmen according to the flesh...
> (Romans 9:3)

An intercessor is able to receive a burden from the Lord about someone or something where He wants His will displayed. The intercessor forgets self and his own needs and identifies with the needs of those for whom he prays.

God seeks intercessors.[30] God seeks anyone who will stand in the gap as Moses did that He might not pour out His wrath.

> I searched for a man among them who would
> build up the wall and stand in the gap before Me
> for the land, so that I would not destroy it; but I
> found no one. (Ezekiel 22:30)

God seeks intercessors that He might bring forth His delivering power as He did through Samuel (1 Samuel 7), Daniel (Daniel 9:16-23), and Moses (Exodus 32:11-23). Intercessors are a rare breed.

> And He saw that there was no man,
> And was astonished that there was no one to intercede;
> Then His own arm brought salvation to Him,
> And His righteousness upheld Him.
> (Isaiah 59:16)

> There is no one who calls on Your name,
> Who arouses himself to take hold of You;
> For You have hidden Your face from us
> And have delivered us into the power of our
> iniquities. (Isaiah 64:7)

Unlike the Great Intercessor, man is too concerned with his own interests and needs to call forth God's blessing upon weary and weak Christian workers and souls headed toward eternal judgment. God longs to dispense miraculous blessings, reveal His mighty arm of power, and display His glory and redemptive love but lacks intercessors to prepare the way.[31] Intercessory prayer reaches its highest power and its highest goal when it is intended to usher in the Kingdom and accomplish the will of God.

The best intercessors look for others with whom they can pray. They are familiar with the lesson Ecclesiastes 4:9-12 teaches:

> Two are better than one because they have a good return for their labor. For if either of them falls, the one will lift up his companion. But woe to the one who falls when there is not another to lift him up. Furthermore, if two lie down together they keep warm, but how can one be warm alone? And if one can overpower him who is alone, two can resist him. A cord of three strands is not quickly torn apart.

Effective intercessors may also inherit what God promises in Leviticus 26:7-8.

> But you will chase your enemies and they will fall before you by the sword; five of you will chase a hundred, and a hundred of you will chase ten thousand, and your enemies will fall before you by the sword.

Those who base their prayers on the Word of God, the sword of the Spirit, will one day discover that the Father used their intercessions to bring to fruition a multitude of victories. One of those blessings will be to defeat the stronghold of selfishness in the one who intercedes according to the will of God.

PERSONAL APPLICATION

1) What is the purpose of intercession?

2) Why is compassion a part of intercessory prayer?

3) What are some of the needs of others that cry out for your prayers?

4) How do you know if God has specifically burdened you to pray for someone or some situation?

5) Do you desire to grow as an intercessor? How will you know if you are growing as an intercessor?

12

PETITION

In that day you will not question Me about anything. Truly, truly, I say to you, if you ask the Father for anything in My name, He will give it to you. Until now you have asked for nothing in My name; ask and you will receive, so that your joy may be made full.
(John 16:23-24)

Prayer is more than responding to God's grace brought to us through the life and ministry of Jesus and the teaching of Scripture. Prayer is also requested for our needs.

Petition is by far the most common element of praying. It is illustrated in the Lord's Prayer by the phrase "give us this day our daily bread" (Matthew 6:11). Because of man's tendency to place asking first, in this section *petition* is listed last because man will not (and should not) forget to ask for his own personal needs even if he forgets all else.

God wants man to ask (Matthew 7:7-8; John 14:13-14; 15:7,16; 16:23-24). He has commanded us to call to Him and He would reveal great and mighty things.

> 'Call to Me and I will answer you, and I will tell you great and mighty things, which you do not know.' (Jeremiah 33:3)

He has said the reason we don't have, is because we do not ask, and yet He does not want man to ask because of selfish motives.

> You lust and do not have; so you commit murder. You are envious and cannot obtain; so you fight and quarrel. You do not have because you do not ask. You ask and do not receive, because you ask with wrong motives, so that you may spend it on your pleasures. You adulteresses, do you not know that friendship with the world is hostility toward God? Therefore whoever wishes to be a friend of the world makes himself an enemy of God. (James 4:2-4)

Therefore, asking according to the will of God is all-important (James 4:15).

> Instead, you ought to say, "If the Lord wills, we will live and also do this or that."

It is not that God is unwilling to supply man's needs, some comforts, and even some desires and must be convinced. God asks the one praying to align themselves with His will in order to receive answers to prayer. God wants to use the Christian's own prayers as part of the process of transforming the believer into the image of His dear Son with whom He is well pleased. This transformation is the far higher purpose of prayer.

God has instructed man to ask before He will answer. Placing the believer in a dependency relationship helps bring the believer more fully into God's will for his life. God commands that you ask, for this is the way to receive. Yet in all of man's asking, the greatest blessings, and the ones God is most ready to grant, are those that bring the believer into Christ-likeness. One should lift up these petitions in total confidence that God will answer them.

> This is the confidence which we have before Him, that, if we ask anything according to His will, He hears us. And if we know that He hears us in whatever we ask, we know that we have the requests which we have asked from Him. (1 John 5:14-15)

Prayer is bowing before a personal Lord and Savior and seeking for Him to fulfill His will through the request. We should not expect that prayer will be answered according to our designs and obtain exactly what is requested. Bless His dear name that God hears and answers in the way that is best for us.

So, we have seen that prayer in Scripture is a broad word and has diverse elements.

> First of all, then, I urge that entreaties and prayers, petitions and thanksgivings, be made on behalf of all men... (1 Timothy 2:1)

In order to more effectively use this sacred privilege, one should learn to break prayer down into its individual elements or categories. It is not necessary to do so with each prayer or each time we pray. Pray as the Spirit leads. Use the pattern or types of prayer taught in these sections as tools to assist you in seeking God's face and finding His favor. For all who will recognize their need and dependency on God, the Father sits waiting to extend His hand of mercy from the throne of grace.

PERSONAL APPLICATION

1) Does God want you to take your personal concerns, anxieties, needs, and sanctified desires before Him?

2) How do you know that He desires you to continually ask, seek, and knock?

3) How is your Christian life and prayer life based on a relationship of dependency on God?

4) In what ways are you dependent upon God in life?

5) In what ways are you dependent upon God in prayer?

6) Does it bother you to be so dependent on God? If yes, why?

Reaching Heaven Through Prayer

13

PRAYING IN JESUS' NAME

*"Whatever you ask in My name, that will I do,
so that the Father may be glorified in the Son.
If you ask Me anything in My name,
I will do it."*
(John 14:13-14)

Prayer is not a right. It is a privilege; a high and awesome one. God is not obligated to hear and answer any prayer. There are prerequisites, however, that open the door of prayer wider. Understanding and abiding by these conditions gives greater fruitfulness to the grand enterprise of prayer. This section, *Reaching Heaven Through Prayer*, touches on five areas that will improve the fruitfulness of your time with God: "Praying in Jesus' Name," "Praying in Faith," "Asking and Receiving," "Unanswered Prayers," and "Conditions for Answered Prayer."

During the last supper with His disciples, our Lord Jesus spoke six times about praying in His name, (John 14:13-14, 15:16, 16:23-27). If our Lord mentioned it so much, at such an important time in His life, asking in His name must hold important significance for His followers.

Jesus was placing an awesome power at His disciples' disposal. He said that if they asked in His name, that they would receive and that their joy would be made full through receiving.

> Until now you have asked for nothing in My name; ask and you will receive, so that your joy may be made full. (John 16:24)

Jesus attaches unconditional terms like "whatever" and "anything" to those who would pray in His name. He most certainly can do this because of who He is and what He has done. Jesus is the name that is above every name!

Closing a prayer with the phrase "In Jesus' name," is the proper way to end prayer, but it is not simply a formula. It is a realization that our prayers must go through Christ to be heard.

> Jesus said to him, "I am the way, and the truth, and the life; no one comes to the Father but through Me. (John 14:6)

But praying in Jesus' name is also more than simply using Him as our representative. Praying in Jesus' name is praying in His character, with His authority, and for His glory. A name stands for or represents the person. When a name is used we immediately recall the person who bears it. Jesus perfectly represents His Father's name to us.

> "I have manifested Your name to the men whom You gave Me out of the world." (John 17:6)

A person's name represents what that person is, how he lives, what he stands for, and what he stands against. The names of

God in the Bible express some aspect of His character. Praying therefore in Jesus' name means we are to pray as His representative. We are characteristically representing Him in His physical absence, praying what He would pray if He were here. This representation is only possible by praying in His Spirit.

Praying in Jesus' name means praying in His authority. It is a prayer grounded not in our merit or favor but in Jesus Christ's merit. No one can approach God on the grounds of their goodness but only on the ground of Jesus' atoning blood.

> Therefore, brethren, since we have confidence to enter the holy place by the blood of Jesus...
> (Hebrews 10:19)

Our name, like our righteousness, is bankrupt before God. God is under no obligation to hear or answer our prayer, *but* He will hear and answer Jesus' request. Praying in Jesus' name is an appeal to His authority. Jesus "opens" the door into God's presence and gives us the right to be heard.[32]

Praying in Jesus' name is to pray for His glory. To use Jesus' name presupposes the surrender of our interests to the interests of Him whom we represent. The work of the Holy Spirit is to glorify Jesus, and prayer in Jesus' name will be inspired by Him and the Holy Spirit will glorify Jesus.

> But when He, the Spirit of truth, comes, He will guide you into all the truth; for He will not speak on His own initiative, but whatever He hears, He will speak; and He will disclose to you what is to come. He will glorify Me, for He will take of Mine and will disclose it to you.
> (John 16:13-14)

As our character aligns with Christ, we represent Him more faithfully on Earth and before His throne. As Jesus' representatives invested with Jesus' character and purpose, we ask with His right and authority to extend His Kingdom here on Earth for His eternal glory. As we yield ourselves to live for His interest and glory, we become more like the Christ we represent who has total access before the Father, and His every prayer is answered.

PERSONAL APPLICATION

1) Is your joy being made full by praying in Jesus' name?

2) Do you think that what makes Jesus joyful would make you joyful also? Why or why not?

3) In your own words, what is praying in Jesus' name?

4) When your name comes up, what do you hope people think and say about you?

5) What was the original meaning or derivation of the name "Christian" (Acts 11:26)?

6) Is the intent of your prayer to glorify Christ? How do you know that it is?

14

PRAYING IN FAITH

And Jesus answered saying to them, "Have faith in God. Truly I say to you, whoever says to this mountain, 'Be taken up and cast into the sea,' and does not doubt in his heart, but believes that what he says is going to happen, it will be granted him. Therefore I say to you, all things for which you pray and ask, believe that you have received them, and they will be granted you."
(Mark 11:22-24)

Prayer must be done in faith. The Bible states that faith-filled praying is able to move mountains. The mountains Jesus refers to, are figurative mountains such as obstacles, difficulties, or dilemmas that block your way or immobilize you from fulfilling God's will in your life or ministry. The prayer of faith removes these mountains. These verses indicate the source and focus of faith, the dependency of faith, and the persistence of faith.

First, faith is to be in God. When we pray we do not need faith in ourselves, nor in our prayers, but in God. Faith is found from looking to God and not in analyzing the mountain. What we, by ourselves, find impossible, faith in God makes possible. Faith is our invitation to God to do as He wishes. Faith rests in God. When one has lived with God and experienced His awesome and unfailing goodness, one can rest in God. God is faithful.

Faith is the substance of things hoped for and the evidence of things not seen (Hebrews 11:1). Faith is standing on the facts of the Word of God which will sustain and give evidence of the things not seen but real. These evidences of faith are based on truth. God's Word is truth. True faith is simply taking God at His Word.

> Therefore, keep up your courage, men, for I believe God that it will turn out exactly as I have been told. (Acts 27:25)

By abiding in His Word, Jesus abides with us. By being obedient to the Word we walk in faith with Jesus. The walk of faith is a walk of obedience to the Word of God.

> If you abide in Me, and My words abide in you, ask whatever you wish, and it will be done for you. My Father is glorified by this, that you bear much fruit, and so prove to be My disciples. (John 15:7-8)

As we walk with Christ through following the direction of His Word we grow in faith. True faith comes from hearing and walking in the Word of God (Romans 10:17). This faith in Jesus takes hold of the Word of God, obeys its commands and precepts, and trusts its promises.

The source of our faith, the Word of God, focuses our faith on Jesus Christ. Faith is found by filling our heart and life with His love, power, and grace. Through the walk of faith, His light shines on our will and heart enabling us to believe. As unbelief is cast down, Christ reigns more gloriously.

Another thought relating to Mark 11:22-24, is *dependency*. The Greek word (αἰτέω) translated "ask or desire" in verse 24, indicates an *asking in dependency*. As one walks by faith in God with the Lord Jesus, one's dependency on self decreases and his dependency on God increases. God-dependency begins when self-dependency ends. God responds to those who ask out of this dependency relationship. Many times it takes sorrows, suffering, afflictions, and brokenness to bring us to the place of self-helplessness and defeat. Yet these very trials open the door for God to provide evidence to support and sustain our faith.

> ...so that the proof of your faith, being more precious than gold which is perishable, even though tested by fire, may be found to result in praise and glory and honor at the revelation of Jesus Christ... (1 Peter 1:7)

To learn faith is to learn dependency on God. And it is only through faith we live a life that is pleasing to God.

> And without faith it is impossible to please Him, for he who comes to God must believe that He is and that He is a rewarder of those who seek Him. (Hebrews 11:6)

Remember, "But the righteous man shall live by faith" (Romans 1:17).

The new life begins by faith in the Lord Jesus Christ, and by faith, our life continues to build on that eternal foundation. Faith is not found in *seeing* but in believing what you have *not* seen.

> ...while we look not at the things which are seen, but at the things which are not seen; for the things which are seen are temporal, but the things which are not seen are eternal.
> (2 Corinthians 4:18)

Faith views the world through God's eyes and comprehends the things invisible to the natural eye. When you come to God for salvation and in prayer, everything depends on faith. The Christian life is a life continuously lived and nurtured by faith in God and His Word.

Dependent asking from a life lived in believing God's promises through His supplied evidences receives answers from God.

> For this reason we also constantly thank God that when you received the word of God which you heard from us, you accepted it not as the word of men, but for what it really is, the word of God, which also performs its work in you who believe. (1 Thessalonians 2:13)

Faith is the golden key that unlocks the doors to the treasures of God. Faith never knocks in vain at mercy's door. Faith finds assurance applied to the heart, by the Holy Spirit, that God keeps His Word. Be assured that God's promises are tried and true and that He will keep His promises to you.

It is not the *size* of our faith that matters, but the *focus* of our faith. A mustard seed of faith in God, demonstrated by a life that is lived with Jesus and in dependence on the Father, brings God's response. Shift the focus of your praying from the mountain to the sufficiency of the Mountain Mover and step forward in obedience to His Word.[33] As you walk with God, your faith will grow, your confidence will increase, and *you will* receive through your dependent asking.

PERSONAL APPLICATION

1) What are some of the obstacles, difficulties, or dilemmas that block your way or immobilize you?

2) Have you been looking more at the *mountain* or more at *God*? What does God's Word say about your concerns?

3) Are you willing to claim God's promise and walk in light of His truth instead of complaining about the size of the mountain?

4) If you apply faith to your challenging situation, what changes of attitude and actions should become more evident in your walk with Jesus?

5) What kind of prayer does Mark 11:24 say God will *not* answer?

6) What is the difference between expecting an answer from God and demanding *our* wishes?

7) What changes of attitude and actions should become more evident in your daily walk by faith with Jesus? What do you think would be a good way to implement one of these changes?

8) How can our faith be increased so that we can confidently ask God for larger answers to our prayers?

15

ASKING AND RECEIVING

"Ask, and it will be given to you; seek, and you will find; knock, and it will be opened to you. For everyone who asks receives, and he who seeks finds, and to him who knocks it will be opened.
(Matthew 7:7-8)

Jesus invites His disciples to ask and promises that if they do, they will receive. In asking, seeking, and knocking we encounter God and form a deeper relationship with Him. In answering prayer, God proves His reality to us and His care for us. We need to pray because God has placed us in a spiritual struggle in which our spiritual life is maintained and moved forward through prayer because prayer secures His working.

Prayer displays mutual dependency. God accomplishes His will on Earth through answering our prayers. We receive answers to prayer in order that we might carry out God's will upon the Earth. In our inner-dependent relationship, God finds fulfillment through giving and we find fulfillment in receiving.

The self-sufficient God depends on our asking to express His will. The one praying depends on God to answer. Prayer is born and developed in this mutually dependent relationship. God, therefore, commands us to ask (αἰτέω) in our dependency upon Him, and He answers so that we might see and experience His will being done. Through answered prayer, God is glorified and we grow in our faith.

The one who asks expects to receive, just like the one who knocks expects a door to open, while the one who is seeking will surely find God's face. We are not to be passive in our relationship with God nor take our relationship with Him for granted. We are to be active and constantly asking for His involvement.

Seeking is actively pursuing God's face and acting in faith after we have asked in faith. It is faith moving out in dependence upon God's response. The thought, "Knock and it will be opened to you," suggests that grace does not come to us easily. It is as though the earnest asker and diligent seeker have been confronted by a closed door. Though God's desire to help is always there, our prevailing in prayer not only strengthens us but deepens us. Through persistence in God's way, God's grace is given, and God's will is accomplished.

PERSONAL APPLICATION

1) Do you find it easy to ask God for things?

2) What are some things you regularly ask God for?

3) Do you consider yourself dependent on God? If so, how? How is God dependent upon you?

4) Do you expect God to answer when you ask? Is this expectation seen in your stepping out in faith to see God accomplish what you have prayed for?

5) Why are we to be persistent in prayer?

6) What are some prayer requests for which you have had to be persistent until they were accomplished?

Note: Passages for further study: Luke 18, Jeremiah 33:3, Matthew 21:22, and James 4:2.

16

UNANSWERED PRAYERS

This is the confidence which we have before Him, that, if we ask anything according to His will, He hears us. And if we know that He hears us in whatever we ask, we know that we have the requests which we have asked from Him.
(1 John 5:14-15)

Why is it that so much that is called prayer is not ever acknowledged or answered by God? You have probably had people say to you, "I tried prayer and it did not work. I had a need and prayed about it. After I'd prayed for a while, nothing happened. I did not see any results. I am disappointed and I don't believe in prayer." If we were honest we would probably all say there are thousands of prayers that go up but very few answers that come down. Why is that? Is prayer a farce, a superstition, something we just con ourselves into and pretend that it works but it really doesn't?

God does not promise to answer everyone's prayers. Scripture is very clear that God completely ignores some people's prayers. What are some of the reasons God appears to not hear us or answer our prayers?

The first reason for unanswered prayer is that we do not seek God above all else. "God wants us to seek Him more than anything else, even more than we seek answers to prayer."[34]

> 'Call to Me and I will answer you, and I will tell you great and mighty things, which you do not know.' (Jeremiah 33:3)

God wants us to call on Him, to be more occupied with the giver than the gift. God is not a means to our end. He is to be our great desire.

If we focus on our immediate needs and desires we forget what God's ultimate priority is for our best life. God's will for us is to be conformed to the image of His Son.

> For those whom He foreknew, He also predestined to become conformed to the image of His Son, so that He would be the firstborn among many brethren... (Romans 8:29)

> Do not lie to one another, since you laid aside the old self with its evil practices, and have put on the new self who is being renewed to a true knowledge according to the image of the One who created him... (Colossians 3:9-10)

His perfect will for us is to grant those things that will accomplish this glorious end.[35] When we desire Him because of who He is, more than because of what He can do, we will fall deeper in love with Him and it will be easier for Him to transform us into Jesus' character and empower us in His work.

The focus of prayer reveals our motives. James said, "You ask and do not receive, because you ask with wrong motives, so that you may spend it on your pleasures" (James 4:3). We must ask ourselves if our desires are for self-interest or if they will ultimately bring glory to God. It is not wrong to ask for daily bread or for the desires of our heart when they are in accordance with God's will for us, but the focus must be on God and that He be glorified by the answer. Some prayers are not answered in spite of being honest desires because they do not bring about God's best interest for us (Matthew 17:1-18, 20:20-23, Luke 9:51-56).

Another reason God withholds answers to our prayers is that the timing is wrong. He does not say *no* but *wait*. Like impatient children, we ask, "Are we there yet?" But in truth, we are not yet ready for His answer. If your five-year-old wanted a pocketknife and a flashlight, you would give him the flashlight knowing he needed to mature before you would trust him with the knife. God is ready to give us the desires of our heart if we have become mature enough to handle them.

> Delight yourself in the Lord;
> And He will give you the desires of your heart.
> (Psalm 37:4)

God may also have us wait because He is planning to do something even better for us than what we asked.

> Now to Him who is able to do far more
> abundantly beyond all that we ask or think,
> according to the power that works within us, to
> Him be the glory in the church and in Christ

Jesus to all generations forever and ever. Amen. (Ephesians 3:20-21)

We have previously discussed being clean before God, abiding in His Word, praying in the Spirit, listening to Him, and being persistent in our requests. Refusing to heed any of these can cause God to be unresponsive to our prayer. We have also learned that we are to pray as a representative of Christ. We are to pray in faith focusing on God and His will. If any of these responsibilities are sidestepped we can short-circuit our direct line to God.

Another reason our prayer may not be answered is that something is wrong in our lives. Perhaps we have set up some barrier between God and ourselves. The next chapter will deal with these and several other types of hindrances to having our prayers answered.

PERSONAL APPLICATION

1) List some of your prayer requests that have not yet been answered.

2) Compare each of these requests with the following criteria:

   - Would it bring glory to God?
   - Would it advance His Kingdom?
   - Would it help people?
   - Would it help me become more Christ-like?

3) Why do you think God wants to transform us into the image of Christ?

4) What are some of your prayer requests to which God has said *no*?

5) Can you now see possible reasons God said *no* to any of these requests?

6) Is it possible God has said *wait* to some of these?

17

CONDITIONS FOR ANSWERED PRAYER

There are certain conditions that the one praying needs to fulfill so God, who is always willing to bless His children, might respond to their prayer.

Those in the nursery cannot hear the worship services without the aid of a sound system to send a direct signal through their speaker. Those in the sanctuary can't hear what is going on in the nursery either because of the barriers that exist between them. Jesus is in heaven at the right hand of the Father, and through Him, every believer has direct access to the throne of grace to make his or her petitions known. But like the walls that hinder speech, a believer's ability to hear from God and for God to hear them is often hindered.

Although your prayer life may not be hindered by *all* the following prayer killers, it takes only one to keep you from receiving an answer from God. Let us look at some ways to remove possible barriers to answered prayer in our lives and get to the heart of the problem.

EXPECT TO RECEIVE WHAT YOU ASK FOR

"And all things you ask in prayer, believing, you will receive." (Matthew 21:22)

Faith is believing that God cares enough to act. Faith sees that God is working with us and not just watching us from afar. Our faith must be placed in God as the One who answers prayer and not in ourselves or in what we are asking. He is a Father who is predisposed to grant what His children ask.

Faith in uttering prayers is claiming God's will and Word. This is not presumption because the presumption is without basis. Claiming our requests that are based on the promises of God which have been affirmed in us by the Holy Spirit, is God's expectation of us.

> But he must ask in faith without any doubting, for the one who doubts is like the surf of the sea, driven and tossed by the wind. For that man ought not to expect that he will receive anything from the Lord, being a double-minded man, unstable in all his ways. (James 1:6-8)

Faith is complete confidence in God. It is a firm trust in, and loyalty to, God. It rests in the faithfulness of God and His Word and expects Him to honor it and our prayers.

> So faith comes from hearing, and hearing by the word of Christ. (Romans 10:17)

ASK ACCORDING TO GOD'S WILL

This is the confidence which we have before Him, that, if we ask anything according to His will, He hears us. And if we know that He hears us in whatever we ask, we know that we have the requests which we have asked from Him. (1 John 5:14-15)

Another declared condition is asking according to God's revealed will. This implies not only asking for such requests as God is willing to grant, but also living in God's revealed will. Proverbs 28:9 says, "He who turns away his ear from listening to the law, even his prayer is an abomination."

ASK SPECIFICALLY

Ask, and it will be given to you; seek, and you will find; knock, and it will be opened to you. For everyone who asks receives, and he who seeks finds, and to him who knocks it will be opened. (Matthew 7:7-8)

To see answers to prayer, we must pray for a specific object, person, or concern. In all cases where the Bible records answers to prayer, the petitioner prayed for a definite object.

> She made a vow and said, "O Lord of hosts, if You will indeed look on the affliction of Your maidservant and remember me, and not forget Your maidservant, but will give Your maidservant a son, then I will give him to the Lord all the days of his life, and a razor shall never come on his head." (1 Samuel 1:11)

It is always more difficult to see answers when we have prayed in generalities.

GENUINENESS

> *He who turns away his ear from listening to the law, even his prayer is an abomination.*
> *(Proverbs 28:9)*

You cannot expect God to hear you if you do not genuinely listen to Him. Whoever will not listen, will not be listened to. This kind of hearing means a willingness to obey what God is saying. Whoever refuses to heed God's Word has no basis for expecting God to answer, but let it be remembered that God is merciful and gracious.

> The sacrifice of the wicked is an abomination to the Lord, but the prayer of the upright is His delight. (Proverbs 15:8)

> The Lord is far from the wicked,
> But He hears the prayer of the righteous.
> (Proverbs 15:29)

UNSELFISHNESS

> *You ask and do not receive, because you ask with wrong motives, so that you may spend it on your pleasures. (James 4:3)*

The motive of our prayer must not be for the glory of self, but for the glory of God. We must ask ourselves if we are more interested in our *own* desires than we are in the glorifying of God.

> I glorified You on the earth, having accomplished the work which You have given Me to do. (John 17:4)

A CLEAR CONSCIENCE

> *We will know by this that we are of the truth, and will assure our heart before Him in whatever our heart condemns us; for God is greater than our heart and knows all things. Beloved, if our heart does not condemn us, we have confidence before God; and whatever we ask we receive from Him, because we keep His commandments and do the things that are pleasing in His sight. (1 John 3:20-22)*

Two things are made plain in these verses. The first is that to prevail with God, we must have a sensitive conscience which readily convicts us of our sin so that we may confess our sin and find cleansing from whatever is offensive to our Father. Second, we must keep Jesus' commandments by doing those things that are pleasing in His sight.

A PURE HEART

> *If I regard wickedness in my heart, The Lord will not hear... (Psalm 66:18)*

Any contaminants in your heart will hinder your praying and keep your Christian life from achieving its full potential. We must be honest and loving in prayer and not harbor iniquity (sin) in our heart. A seeker with a pure heart will have a proper attitude and right actions. He or she walks in integrity.

CONFESSION AND RESTITUTION

> *He who conceals his transgressions will not prosper, but he who confesses and forsakes them will find compassion. (Proverbs 28:13)*

An unwillingness to acknowledge our sins and make our sins right with God and others hinders prayer.

CLEAN HANDS

> *Therefore I want the men in every place to pray, lifting up holy hands, without wrath and dissension. (1 Timothy 2:8)*

> *I shall wash my hands in innocence, And I will go about Your altar, O Lord... (Psalm 26:6)*

The daily works of a person, represented by their hands, must be pure before God.

RECONCILIATION AMONG BELIEVERS

> *Therefore if you are presenting your offering at the altar, and there remember that your*

> brother has something against you, leave your offering there before the altar and go; first be reconciled to your brother, and then come and present your offering. (Matthew 5:23-24)

Settling disputes and animosities among believers is a condition for answered prayer. Scripture is full of verses supporting God's desire for unity and peace among believers. (John 13:34; I Peter 3:7, 2:13).

HUMILITY

> But He gives a greater grace. Therefore it says, "God is opposed to the proud, but gives grace to the humble." (James 4:6)

A humble God respects a broken and contrite (sensitive to sin) heart.

REMOVAL OF STUMBLING BLOCKS

> "Son of man, these men have set up their idols in their hearts and have put right before their faces the stumbling block of their iniquity. Should I be consulted by them at all?"
> Ezekiel 14:3

An idol is anything in your life that you are putting ahead of God. Is there anything you would not give up for God? If so, you have fashioned an idol. If there are things you won't release to God's control, they may be blocking your access to Him.

FORGIVENESS

And forgive us our debts, as we also have forgiven our debtors. (Matthew 6:12)

But if you do not forgive others, then your Father will not forgive your transgressions. (Matthew 6:15)

God works in your *present* for your future, while the enemy works out of your *past* to affect your present and your future. UN-forgiveness of the past gives the enemy room to work in your present. Forgiveness gives God access to work on your life for His purposes. Ask yourself these questions to reveal whether or not you suffer from UN-forgiveness:

Can you talk about the negative event in your past without getting emotional?

Can you pray for the person or with the person with whom you had the negative encounter? (See I John 2:9-11; Ephesians 4:30-32; Hebrews 12:14-15)

CLEANSING FROM SIN

*Behold, the Lord's hand is not so short
That it cannot save;
Nor is His ear so dull
That it cannot hear.
But your iniquities have made a separation
between you and your God,
And your sins have hidden His face from you
so that He does not hear. (Isaiah 59:1-2)*

Un-confessed sin is probably the most common prayer killer, which is why so many of these conditions touch on some aspect of sin. Psalm 66:18 says, "If I regard wickedness in my heart, the Lord will not hear." Wickedness is Un-confessed and Un-repented sin. Sinfulness separates us from God and God from us. If we knowingly tolerate sin in our lives it pushes us away from God. As a result, our prayers can be powerless. The good news is that if we confess sin, God forgives it and restores the relationship.

> They will not teach again, each man his neighbor and each man his brother, saying, 'Know the Lord,' for they will all know Me, from the least of them to the greatest of them," declares the Lord, "for I will forgive their iniquity, and their sin I will remember no more." (Jeremiah 31:34)

PRAYING IN CHRIST'S NAME

> *Whatever you ask in My name, that will I do, so that the Father may be glorified in the Son. If you ask Me anything in My name, I will do it. (John 14:13-14)*

> *In that day you will not question Me about anything. Truly, truly, I say to you, if you ask the Father for anything in My name, He will give it to you. Until now you have asked for nothing in My name; ask and you will receive, so that your joy may be made full. (John 16:23-24)*

> *Jesus said to him, "I am the way, and the truth, and the life; no one comes to the Father but through Me." (John 14:6)*

> *Therefore, brethren, since we have confidence to enter the holy place by the blood of Jesus... (Hebrews 10:19)*

A name stands for or represents the person. When a name is used we immediately recall the person who bears it.

> *"I have manifested Your name to the men whom You gave Me out of the world; they were Yours and You gave them to Me, and they have kept Your word." (John 17:6)*

A name represents who that person is, how he lives, and what he stands for or against. When we pray in Jesus' name, we are praying as His representative. We are characteristically representing Him in His physical absence, and praying what He would pray if He was here.

INSPIRATION OF THE HOLY SPIRIT

> *In the same way the Spirit also helps our weakness; for we do not know how to pray as we should, but the Spirit Himself intercedes for us with groanings too deep for words; and He who searches the hearts knows what the mind of the Spirit is, because He intercedes for the saints according to the will of God. (Romans 8:26-27)*

> The end of all things is near; therefore, be of sound judgment and sober spirit for the purpose of prayer. *(1 Peter 4:7)*

> But you, beloved, building yourselves up on your most holy faith, praying in the Holy Spirit... *(Jude 20)*

> With all prayer and petition pray at all times in the Spirit, and with this in view, be on the alert with all perseverance and petition for all the saints... *(Ephesians 6:18)*

> "I will pour out on the house of David and on the inhabitants of Jerusalem, the Spirit of grace and of supplication, so that they will look on Me whom they have pierced; and they will mourn for Him, as one mourns for an only son, and they will weep bitterly over Him like the bitter weeping over a firstborn." *(Zechariah 12:10)*

All true prayer is inspired by and led by the Holy Spirit. Your relationship toward God must be one of deep dependence and utter submission.

FERVENCY

> Therefore, confess your sins to one another, and pray for one another so that you may be healed. The effective prayer of a righteous man can accomplish much. *(James 5:16)*

Persevering and prevailing prayer is essential. Half-hearted prayer is self-defeating.

HONOR YOUR WIFE

> *You husbands in the same way, live with your wives in an understanding way, as with someone weaker, since she is a woman; and show her honor as a fellow heir of the grace of life, so that your prayers will not be hindered.*
> *(1 Peter 3:7)*

How we treat others can hinder our prayers. God expects us to resolve relational conflicts (Matthew 5:23-24; 1 John 2:9). Unresolved horizontal strife closes the vertical connection. Harmonious relationships with God's children opens up and deepens God's relationship with us. Matthew 18:15 tells us how to be reconciled. If a reconciliation attempt is not received, don't worry.

> *If possible, so far as it depends on you, be at peace with all men.* (Romans 12:18)

As we respond to God and His Word, we will be entrusted with the powerful resources that come to us through answered prayer. If you meet these conditions and you are a child of God, you have every right to expect that God will answer your prayer. He may not always answer with an immediate *yes*. It may be *wait* or even *no* because He is working for our eternal good, but in grace and love, He will answer His children.

PERSONAL APPLICATION

1) Which of these 18 conditions to answered prayer give you the most trouble? Which are not as difficult for you?

2) This list of hindrances to prayer is not complete. Brainstorm about some other prayer killers.

   Example:

   He who shuts his ear to the cry of the poor will also cry himself and not be answered.
   (Proverbs 21:13)

3) Now is the time to take each unanswered prayer to our Father and ask Him why He is not responding. If you listen, He may reveal the root cause.

A Prayer Warrior's Armor
(part 1)

18

SPIRITUAL ARMOR

Finally, be strong in the Lord and in the strength of His might. Put on the full armor of God, so that you will be able to stand firm against the schemes of the devil.
(Ephesians 6:10-11)

The Christian is asked in Ephesians 6:11 "to stand firm against the schemes of the devil." Here the word *schemes* carry the idea of being shrewd, crafty, and deceitful, and could be translated *insidious* or *treacherous* schemes. The Greek word (μεθοδείας) was frequently used to describe an indomitable animal that is crafty and unexpectedly attacks its victims. Likewise, the schemes of the devil are constructed to deceive and injure. They are prepared to be launched when you are spiritually weak, or to catch you at an "opportune" time.

When the devil had finished every temptation,
he left Him until an *opportune* time. (Luke 4:13)

Our ultimate foe is not "flesh and blood" but supernatural and his skillful methodical attack is from the spiritual realm with ancient evil power. We must protect ourselves with spiritual armor in order to withstand Satan's insidious attacks and stand firm so that God might use us to defeat his schemes. Spiritual armor is needed so that the Christian might stand firm in the spiritual battle.

> For our struggle is not against flesh and blood,
> but against the rulers, against the powers,
> against the world forces of this darkness, against
> the spiritual forces of wickedness in the
> heavenly places. (Ephesians 6:12)

The word *against,* that proceeds each supernatural power, separates a particular demonic activity and level of authority within the kingdom of Satan. The forces of darkness are highly organized, specialized, and structured for the most destructive impact possible. The Greek word translated *fight* was used for hand-to-hand combat. It was frequently used to describe a life and death struggle. Satan is out to steal, kill, and destroy your spiritual life.

> The thief comes only to steal and kill and
> destroy; I came that they may have life, and
> have it abundantly. (John 10:10)

Whether you know it or not, you are in a life and death battle for your Christian life. Yes, spiritual life is a war. Our weakness in prayer is the result of neglecting this truth.[36]

PERSONAL APPLICATION

1) What is spiritual warfare?

2) Who is our real enemy?

3) Have you ever felt like you were in a spiritual battle? What was that like?

4) How do we win this type of battle?

19

THE BELT OF TRUTH

*Stand firm therefore,
having girded your loins with truth...
(Ephesians 6:14)*

The pieces of the Christian warrior's armor are listed in various places throughout the Bible but they are concentrated in Ephesians 6:13-18. In the next six chapters, we will look at each piece to gain a greater understanding of their purpose and usefulness. The first piece of the battle gear listed is the belt of truth.

> Jesus said to him, "I am the way, and the truth, and the life; no one comes to the Father but through Me." (John 14:6)

Soldiers in His army must be faithful or true to Him and to His ideals. As children of the light, we must love and live the truth. Our lives must be free of any falseness or hypocrisy. Jesus lives in you, therefore the truth is in you. Yet you are not always going to choose the way of truth if you do not abide in the Word of truth—the Holy Scriptures.

> If you keep My commandments, you will abide
> in My love; just as I have kept My Father's
> commandments and abide in His love.
> (John 15:10)

Christ prayed, "Sanctify them in the truth, Thy Word is truth" (John 17:17). The truth is the only authority that God will support. The Bible is the truth.

> Be diligent to present yourself approved to God
> as a workman who does not need to be
> ashamed, accurately handling the word of truth.
> (2 Timothy 2:15)

> In the exercise of His will He brought us forth
> by the word of truth, so that we would be a kind
> of first fruits among His creatures. (James 1:18)

We must accept the Bible as the truth, as the only and final authority, without error when originally written.

Satan is the promoter of lies, and he uses lies so that we might fall under the power of his kingdom.

> You are of your father the devil, and you want to
> do the desires of your father. He was a murderer
> from the beginning, and does not stand in the
> truth because there is no truth in him.
> Whenever he speaks a lie, he speaks from his
> own nature, for he is a liar and the father of lies.
> (John 8:44)

The believer that is controlled by the Holy Spirit actively embraces Jesus and His Word of truth as His protection against the deception of the devil. The loins represent the originating place of strong desires and longings. We gird our loins with truth so that our desires and longings, both material and sensual, are protected, cleansed, and controlled by God's truth.

The Roman soldier would cinch his belt in order to keep the breastplate in place and to support the back and protect the kidneys. The belt was placed over the tunic, tucking the ends of the tunic under the belt for greater mobility and in preparation for action or work. The sword was also attached to the belt to keep it close to the body.

The thick leather belt was not an offensive weapon but provided support and protection. When we practice the truth daily, its support and protection cause us to love truth more and more until we live with such transparent honesty that we give no place for the enemy. God's truth keeps us from being deceived and from deceiving ourselves. Living in the truth frees us from the destructive debilitating lies of Satan. If we do not believe his lies, we are not under his power and he does not have an open door to do damage to us or through us. Girding ourselves with God's truth will not prevent our being attacked by lies or liars, but it will protect the believer from being destroyed by them.

PERSONAL APPLICATION

1) What is God's truth?

2) Is God's truth important enough for you to gird up your loins with truth daily?

3) How do you gird yourself with truth?

4) What is the devil's primary weapon against God's truth?

5) Are Satan's attacks against you planned or accidental? Can you withstand them using your own defenses and skills?

6) Who is the final authority in your life? How do you know?

7) What is the belt of truth designated to protect? What does this part of the body represent to you?

8) Are you having difficulty with your desires or longings concerning sensuality or material things?

9) Are these problems within our culture? How has our culture fallen for Satan's lies?

10) What is the purpose of spiritual armor?

11) What are some of the ways Christians are like soldiers?

12) Are you aware of any schemes of the devil operating in your life today?

20

THE BREASTPLATE OF RIGHTEOUSNESS

...put on the breastplate of righteousness...
(Ephesians 6:14)

Another essential part of the soldier's equipment was the *breastplate* made of metal plates, chain links or shaped metal. It covered the soldier's torso from the neck to below the waist, both front and back. The breastplate protected vital organs like the heart, lungs, and intestines. The Jews called the intestines entrails or bowels. The entrails symbolized the emotions because of the way the stress and strains of our emotions affect the digestive organs. The heart frequently represented our affections and will, and was thought of as the seat of our intellect. Even the intentions and attitudes of the temperament or disposition were thought to be lodged in the heart. In order to protect these vital areas of life, we need to put on the breastplate of righteousness.

On the day of our salvation, we surrendered our life to the Lord Jesus Christ. On that day, God justified us by placing the righteousness of Jesus Christ to our account. The justification of Jesus was imputed to us as a legal act by the Father.

> More than that, I count all things to be loss in view of the surpassing value of knowing Christ Jesus my Lord, for whom I have suffered the loss of all things, and count them but rubbish so that I may gain Christ, and may be found in Him, not having a righteousness of my own derived from the Law, but that which is through faith in Christ, the righteousness which comes from God on the basis of faith...
> (Philippians 3:8-9)

Positional or imputed righteousness can occur because God placed all our sins upon Christ and charged *Him* with *our* sins. God then punished his Son for our sins on the cross. He "who knew no sin became sin for us so that we might become the righteousness of God in Him" (2 Corinthians 5:21). This is the reason God turned His back on His Son.

> About the ninth hour Jesus cried out with a loud voice, saying, "Eli, Eli, lama sabachthani?" that is, "My God, My God, why have You forsaken Me?" (Matthew 27:46)

God also takes the righteousness of Christ and accounts it as ours (Romans 3:24-25; 4:25; 5:18, 2 Corinthians 5:21, 1 John 3:5). Justification is God's act of grace when He declares the believer just, by the acts and merits of Jesus Christ. Our position before the Judge of the Universe is one of vindication in the shed blood of Jesus. Our refuge against the attacks of the accuser is that we are justified by the imparted righteousness of Christ. This justification is an unalterable historical event. The righteousness of Christ is not only over us, but it is also *in* us because Jesus, who is our righteousness, lives within each person who has surrendered to His Lordship.

As the righteousness of Christ is properly worn, it produces holy living and God's righteousness protects the spiritual warrior's life. Even though we are positionally saints, it does not mean we are conditionally righteous or completely sanctified, and we will not be until the return of Jesus.

> For I am confident of this very thing, that He who began a good work in you will perfect it until the day of Christ Jesus. (Philippians 1:6)
>
> Beloved, now we are children of God, and it has not appeared as yet what we will be. We know that when He appears, we will be like Him, because we will see Him just as He is. And everyone who has this hope fixed on Him purifies himself, just as He is pure.
> (1 John 3:2-3)

In order to develop personal holiness, we must win the internal war to follow God's will and way. The battle to develop experiential holiness is an intense daily fight. Satan looks for a weak area in the believer's spiritual armor so that he might exploit it. Without personal sanctification, vital areas in the believer's life will be vulnerable.

> ...and put on the new self, which in the likeness of God has been created in righteousness and holiness of the truth. (Ephesians 4:24)

If there are problems in the vital areas of the emotions, priorities, attitudes, or actions, there is a problem properly putting on the breastplate of righteousness. If your ambitions, decencies, loyalties, or affections are incorrect, you are vulnerable and the enemy has entrance into your life to devour, exploit, and destroy.

The process of sanctification occurs through daily obedience to the revealed will of God for your life. God has provided the breastplate of righteousness to protect the vital areas of our spiritual lives, but we are responsible to dress ourselves in the righteousness of Christ by our own desire for personal sanctification. In the Christian's battle against enemy forces, righteousness, or integrity (Proverbs 28:6, 18) and a pure life, are armor for keeping an enemy spear from hitting you directly in the heart of your life.

> ...in all things show yourself to be an example of good deeds, with purity in doctrine, dignified, sound in speech which is beyond reproach, so that the opponent will be put to shame, having nothing bad to say about us. (Titus 2:7-8)

PERSONAL APPLICATION

1) What does Isaiah 64:6 say about our righteousness without Christ?

2) What is imputed righteousness?

3) What can the heart symbolize in Scriptures?

4) Are these vital areas in your life? Why or why not?

5) How do you put on Christ's righteousness practically?

6) What is personal sanctification?

7) Why is personal holiness important?

8) Read Hebrews 12: 9-14:

> Furthermore, we had earthly fathers to discipline us, and we respected them; shall we not much rather be subject to the Father of spirits, and live? For they disciplined us for a short time as seemed best to them, but He disciplines us for our good, so that we may share His holiness. All discipline for the moment seems not to be joyful, but sorrowful; yet to those who have been trained by it, afterwards it

yields the peaceful fruit of righteousness. Therefore, strengthen the hands that are weak and the knees that are feeble, and make straight paths for your feet, so that the limb which is lame may not be put out of joint, but rather be healed. Pursue peace with all men, and the sanctification without which no one will see the Lord.

21

THE SHOES OF PEACE

...and having shod your feet with the preparation of the gospel of peace...
(Ephesians 6:15)

The Roman soldier's shoes had thick reinforced nail-studded soles. The metal nail protrusions helped give the warrior greater stability and quickness of movement. The shoes covered from the middle of the lower leg down, with wide strips of leather that securely fixed the shoes to the soles of the feet. They were fitted securely to facilitate the rapid, non-slip foot movement necessary for hand-to-hand combat.

The ability to stand firm without slipping or falling was a great help, especially in battle. The soldier who lost his footing could lose his life. The Christian, with his feet firmly planted in the gospel of peace, will have confidence and assurance when he confronts the enemy of the Christ-filled life. To attempt to stand against the enemy on any other ground than the gospel of Jesus Christ is precarious footing sure to cause defeat.

The gospel is the way of peace with God because it is *from* God. When you receive Christ you are united with the Prince of Peace. To walk after the way of Christ is to put on the sandals of peace. "He is our peace" (Ephesians 2:13-14a). Every true Christian has positional peace with God both now and always.

> Therefore, having been justified by faith, we have peace with God through our Lord Jesus Christ, through whom also we have obtained our introduction by faith into this grace in which we stand; and we exult in hope of the glory of God. (Romans 5:1-2)

This peace is objective and legal for we have been justified by God through Jesus Christ and are no longer an enemy to Him. God changed our position from enemies to adopted sons and daughters when we placed our faith in the death, burial, and resurrection of Jesus Christ.

> Much more then, having now been justified by His blood, we shall be saved from the wrath of God through Him. For if while we were enemies we were reconciled to God through the death of His Son, much more, having been reconciled, we shall be saved by His life. (Romans 5:9-10)

No one or nothing can change this reconciliatory positional peace with God through His Gospel. The Christian can lose his *relational* peace though, by not daily walking in the straight-and-narrow path of the gospel.

The peace of Christ must rule in our hearts if we are going to experience the *relational* or *conditional* peace of God which surpasses all comprehension and guards our hearts and minds in Christ Jesus (Philippians 4:5-8). This peace does not depend on our circumstances but on our relationship with Jesus Christ. When we permit the Word of God to reign in our life abundantly, we will have such peace.

> Let the peace of Christ rule in your hearts, to which indeed you were called in one body; and be thankful. Let the word of Christ richly dwell within you, with all wisdom teaching and admonishing one another with psalms and hymns and spiritual songs, singing with thankfulness in your hearts to God.
> (Colossians 3:15-16)

When we walk in submission to Christ, we walk in obedience and we walk in His peace.

A soldier must be trained and prepared for his work and the Christian soldier must be trained and prepared to share the good news of peace with God to others. We call it the "gospel of peace" because it can destroy the hostility that resides in man and replace it with the tranquility of God.

> How lovely on the mountains
> Are the feet of him who brings good news,
> Who announces peace
> And brings good news of happiness,
> Who announces salvation,
> And says to Zion, "Your God reigns!"
> (Isaiah 52:7)

Each day we must be ready to share the gospel of peace. As ambassadors of peace, we share the good news with those who do not personally know Jesus so that they can establish a relationship with Him and walk in His path of peace.

> Therefore if anyone is in Christ, he is a
> new creature; the old things passed away;
> behold, new things have come. Now all these
> things are from God, who reconciled us to
> Himself through Christ and gave us the ministry
> of reconciliation, namely, that God was in Christ
> reconciling the world to Himself, not counting
> their trespasses against them, and He has
> committed to us the word of reconciliation.
> Therefore, we are ambassadors for Christ,
> as though God were making an appeal through
> us; we beg you on behalf of Christ, be reconciled
> to God. He made Him who knew no sin to be sin
> on our behalf, so that we might become the
> righteousness of God in Him.
> (2 Corinthians 5:17-21)

There are persons and families living in the agony of anger, deception, fear, and mistrust. God wants to establish His reign of forgiveness, reconciliation, and peace in all these difficult situations.

Those who walk in the peace of God also reach out to restore peace in relationships among the brethren. The accuser of the brethren practices the old proverb "divide and conquer" and provokes dissension, distortions, distrust, and disloyalty in the army of God. His demons use rumors, cursing, misinterpretation of facts, and suppositions to separate those within the local church. But those who walk in the peace of the gospel *calm the roar of the lion* in situations and lives by applying the Word of peace.

> Let the peace of Christ rule in your hearts, to
> which indeed you were called in one body; and be
> thankful. Let the word of Christ richly dwell
> within you, with all wisdom teaching and

admonishing one another with psalms and hymns and spiritual songs, singing with thankfulness in your hearts to God. (Colossians 3:15-16)

We cannot give to others what we do not possess ourselves. If we live in the peace of profound fellowship with Jesus, we can jump into the battle with settled determination and calm security of our position. A soldier who cannot maintain their footing is useless in battle. Similarly, the Christian who does not walk in the gospel of peace is useless in a *spiritual* battle.

The Christian soldier fights to establish the *peace of God*, not to make war. He fights against the malignant in order to bring the healing peace of God to persons and situations. Satan is the principal cause of agitation and division in the world. The peacemaking Christian makes peace by opposing Satan and his works, and by promoting reconciliation and fellowship with God and man. The peacemakers can claim the promise that "the God of Peace will soon crush Satan under your feet" (Romans 16:20).

PERSONAL APPLICATION

1) Why do you think the "gospel of peace" was compared to footwear?

2) What is *positional* peace with God? What is *conditional* peace with God?

3) Do you think you can truly be a "peacemaker" if you are not prepared to share Jesus Christ with those around you?

4) What are two ways Christians can bring peace as they walk through their daily life?

5) What is an old strategy the devil uses to get his way in an individual's and church's life? How have you seen this tactic used in the church?

6) Have you ever lived *without* daily peace guarding your heart and mind? What brought about this loss of peace?

7) Are you walking daily in the peace of God now? How do you know?

8) When was the last time you helped someone find peace with God?

A Prayer Warrior's Armor
(part 2)

22

THE SHIELD OF FAITH

*...in addition to all, taking up the shield of faith
with which you will be able to extinguish all
the flaming arrows of the evil one.
(Ephesians 6:16)*

The next three pieces of spiritual armor—the Shield of Faith, the Helmet of Salvation, and the Sword of the Spirit—appear to be distinguished from the first three pieces soldiers put on at the beginning of each day. The reintroduction of the verb "take" or "take up" (from verse 13) indicates that the shield, helmet, and sword were carried along in readiness for the battle.[37] Placing the phrase "in addition to all" also divides the pieces here. "In addition to all" seems to indicate that faith is necessary with regard to all the pieces of the Christian's armor. This shield consisting of faith would be employed to protect all the other pieces of armor.

The Roman shield (θυρεόν, which originally meant *door*) refers to a large (4½ feet long by 2½ feet wide) rectangular shield. It was constructed of wood and edged with iron. The shield was covered on the outside with either metal or leather. The metal covering deflected arrows and the treated leather would extinguish the fiery pitch on the arrows. The large size provided considerable protection for the body and fulfilled a strategic role. Interlocking hooks were attached to the sides, which could be locked together to form a wall that would help keep the line from breaking in an attack or during an advance. In our fight of faith, we also need to unite ourselves in faith against the fiery attacks of the adversary (Philippians 1:27). When the church unites in faith even the gates of hell cannot stand against it, and with faith, the church can advance into the territory of the enemy.

> Simon Peter answered, "You are the Christ, the Son of the living God." And Jesus said to him, "Blessed are you, Simon Barjona, because flesh and blood did not reveal this to you, but My Father who is in heaven. I also say to you that you are Peter, and upon this rock I will build My church; and the gates of Hades will not overpower it. I will give you the keys of the kingdom of heaven; and whatever you bind on earth shall have been bound in heaven, and whatever you loose on earth shall have been loosed in heaven." (Matthew 16:16-19)

One of the most dangerous arms of ancient combat was an arrow that had tar or some other combustible material attached to its point. Lit before they were shot, these arrows could not only wound, but they could also ignite and burn. Satan, the evil one, often wars against Christ, His church, and its members by firing flaming arrows of malignancy. These fiery arrows are shot at the heart, mind, and body. They come to us as thoughts, situations, and desires to sin. They are flaming missiles of lies, unbelief, blasphemies, hates, doubts, fears, worries, discouragement, envies, conceits, sensuality, and selfishness to name but a few. The bombarding with these flaming projectiles should awaken us to the scheming craftiness of our adversary's nature and methods. He desires not only to hurt us but also to preoccupy and distract us with his inner and outer fiery eruptions. His plan is to keep us occupied with the fires his arrows create so that we fix our attention on *them* instead of Jesus Christ and the advancement of His Kingdom. If we do not extinguish these burning darts by faith in Jesus Christ, they will injure not only our ministry but also our life.

The shield against the blazing arrows is faith in Jesus Christ and His Word. 2 Samuel 22:31 affirms, "As for God, His way is blameless; The word of the Lord is tested; He is a shield to all who take refuge in Him." God is the object of our faith. He is our shield (Genesis 15:1, Psalm 3:3, 115:9-11, 119:114, and Proverbs 2:7). Trusting in the God of sovereignty, goodness, and faithfulness is the way the believer appropriates His shield. "Faith is trusting completely and unconditionally in God and His Word."[38] You must understand that this faith is confidence in God and His Word because it is not *faith* that protects us, but *God and our obedience to His Word* that protects us.

How did Jesus extinguish the fiery missiles of the father of lies? He answered each shot with the Word of God (see Matthew 4:1-11). When a provocative thought, a hot accusation, or a flaming temptation enters we must come against it with the Word of God. Every time you truly read the Word, listen to a sermon, study the Bible, or memorize a Scripture you fortify your shield of faith. "So faith comes by hearing, and hearing by the word of Christ" (Romans 10:17).

For our Christian growth, God allows some arrows to test us so that our faith in Him and His Word might increase.

When those blazing missiles come, have faith in God and demonstrate it by being obedient to His Word and He will extinguish them in His time.

PERSONAL APPLICATION

1) What was the purpose of the Roman soldier's shield?

2) In what way is faith like a shield? Read Proverbs 30:5.

3) Do you think that the choice of this particular shield, which could be unified with other shields, has any significance for Christian warfare? How?

4) What fiery arrows of Satan has he used to attack you and how did you deal with them?

5) What problems, difficulties, or distractions has your church encountered while serving the Lord? How has your spiritual life or your church progressed when it has been at work putting out fires?

6) Who is our faith in and how do we demonstrate our faith?

7) See Matthew 4:1-11. How did Jesus defend Himself against Satan's attacks?

8) How did Jesus shield Himself throughout His life? Read Proverbs 30:5.

23

THE HELMET OF SALVATION

And take the helmet of salvation...
(Ephesians 6:17)

If the shield was being used in the proper manner to protect the body, the enemy would first attack the head. The fifth of God's armor is therefore of vital importance. The Roman helmet was made of solid metal or of leather with metal reinforcements that would help protect the head from arrows and sword blows. Blows to the head are deadly without a protective helmet properly in place. Just as a soldier is foolish not to protect such a vital and vulnerable area, so is the spiritual warrior.

Those who have enlisted in the Kingdom of God take up the helmet of salvation when they appropriate (to take hold of by faith and make it one's own) the mind of Christ. This helmet saves us from our vain or fleshly manner of thinking. Believers receive the mind of Christ when they receive Jesus as Lord and Savior of their life.

> For who has known the mind of the Lord, that he will instruct Him? But we have the mind of Christ. (1 Corinthians 2:16)

Yet the actual *experiencing* of the mind of Christ only occurs when, by the mercy of God, we surrender our intellectual processing of thought to Him and walk in the will of the Head of the church. Through surrender to Christ, our mind is not only guarded against evil but also transformed so that we can prove that the will of God is good, acceptable, and perfect.

> Therefore I urge you, brethren, by the mercies of God, to present your bodies a living and holy sacrifice, acceptable to God, which is your spiritual service of worship. And do not be conformed to this world, but be transformed by the renewing of your mind, so that you may prove what the will of God is, that which is good and acceptable and perfect. (Romans 12:1-2)

Living life by the mind of Christ enables us to perceive, comprehend, and discern the will of God in the circumstances of our daily life. It enables us to understand, learn, and apply the Word of God. It renews us so that the voice of the Holy Spirit is clearer and clarifies our thinking so that we can walk in agreement with Him.

> Your word is a lamp to my feet
> And a light to my path. (Psalm 119:105)

If we study, learn, and practice the principles of Scripture we are not deceived or detoured. The devil casts his missiles of thought at our mind in order to stimulate fleshly thoughts, and capture our mind with his lies. If we accept his ideas and priorities he can sidetrack our lives. The believer though, who walks in daily submission to the will of God, guards his thoughts by taking them captive to the obedience of Christ (2 Corinthians 10:5).

Another reason for us to firmly place the helmet into position is that it brings security concerning our eternal salvation. Our mind needs divine protection so that we do not doubt the salvation that we freely received by the grace of God. Our salvation is real and eternal.

> Who will separate us from the love of Christ? Will tribulation, or distress, or persecution, or famine, or nakedness, or peril, or sword? Just as it is written,
>
>> "For Your sake we are being put to death all day long; We were considered as sheep to be slaughtered."
>
> But in all these things we overwhelmingly conquer through Him who loved us. For I am convinced that neither death, nor life, nor angels, nor principalities, nor things present, nor things to come, nor powers, nor height, nor depth, nor any other created thing, will be able to separate us from the love of God, which is in Christ Jesus our Lord. (Romans 8:35-39)

Satan can cast doubts so that we question the reality of salvation and sometimes even our own personal salvation. If we walk in doubt we cannot walk in faith, and faith is our victory over the world (1 John 5:4). There can be times when a Christian will even think that after falling into temptation and sin, they do not deserve their salvation, and this is true, but it is not the complete truth. We are not saved because we deserve it. We are saved because we placed our faith in Jesus Christ and what He did for us on the cross, and by grace, God justifies us or gives us a right to stand before Him. God transferred us from the kingdom of darkness into the kingdom of light. Since we did not *earn* it, we cannot *unearn* it. Salvation is a gift of God not the reward of works.

We have been made positionally righteous before God. Our conditional unrighteousness costs us fellowship and sanctification—not salvation. We presently have eternal salvation, not a *chance* at eternal salvation.

> My sheep hear My voice, and I know them, and they follow Me; and I give eternal life to them, and they will never perish; and no one will snatch them out of My hand. My Father, who has given them to Me, is greater than all; and no one is able to snatch them out of the Father's hand. (John 10:27-29)
>
> These things I have written to you who believe in the name of the Son of God, so that you may know that you have eternal life. (1 John 5:13)

Take up the helmet of salvation in Christ Jesus. Believe His Word that declares that if you have been saved, you have been eternally, irrevocably saved (Romans 8:35-39; John 10:26-30). Protect and sanctify your mind through systematically studying, meditating, and memorizing the Word of God. Take what you learn, put it into practice, "And the peace of God, which surpasses all comprehension, will guard your hearts and your minds in Christ Jesus (Philippians 4:6-9).

PERSONAL APPLICATION

1) Appropriate means to take hold of by faith and make it one's own. What does the thought, "Appropriate the mind of Christ by taking up the helmet of salvation," mean to you?

2) Respond to the thought that assurance is the birthright of every believer.

3) Why do you think Satan would want us to doubt the reality of our salvation?

4) Has the devil ever confused you, depressed you, or tempted you into doubting your salvation? How did you deal with it?

5) Why do you think those who are not being sanctified or transformed into the image of Jesus by their daily walk with God, would doubt their salvation?

6) Did you save yourself or did the Lord save you? How did God save you? Read Romans 8:16. "The Spirit himself bears witness with our spirit that we are children of God." Does the Spirit bear witness with you that you are a child of God? Do you think that you are saved eternally

or that you only have received a chance for eternal salvation?

24

THE SWORD OF THE SPIRIT

*...and the sword of the Spirit,
which is the word of God.
(Ephesians 6:17)*

The Greek word translated "sword" refers to a finely honed, double-edged, short sword (Matthew 26:47; 10:34). Roman soldiers practiced frequently with this sword because their life depended on perfecting its use. The warrior must be strong, quick, and dexterous to use this weapon intended to thrust and penetrate.

The *Belt of Truth*, the *Breastplate of Righteousness*, and the *Shoes of Peace* are defensive pieces of armor, and all the experienced warrior has to be concerned about is putting them on properly. The *Sword of the Spirit*, though, is both defensive and offensive, and like any other sword, training is needed in order to use it effectively. It is the only offensive weapon of the armor, but no other is necessary. There must be no doubt that the divine Word is adequate because it is without error or fault, perfect and impeccable.

The Greek word used here for Word is *rhema*, not *logos*. Paul is definitely referring to the written Word of God. It was the written Word that Jesus used to defeat Satan when He was tempted in the wilderness. Three times Jesus, in a loud voice, replied to Satan "it is written" and then quoted from memory a Scripture verse (Matthew 4:1-11). Yet on the same occasion, Satan misquoted and misinterpreted Scripture also. This practice of misusing Scripture is still used today by various groups. The Christian must know the Word of God and be trained in how to use it as his spiritual weapon. The more familiar you are with the Word, the easier it is to detect the lies of Lucifer and the more effective you can be at rejecting his temptations.

Martin Luther learned to use the Word to defeat the devil and he proclaimed the Word's value in his hymn, *A Mighty Fortress is Our God*.

> "And though this world, with devils filled,
>   should threaten to undo us,
> We will not fear, for God hath willed His truth to
>   triumph through us."

The better we know and treasure the Word of God in our hearts, the better we can use it as Jesus modeled for us. Though difficult, the study and memorization of Scripture are necessary for each disciple. As you study and memorize the Bible you will discover its profound significance.

> For the word of God is living and active and sharper than any two-edged sword, and piercing as far as the division of soul and spirit, of both joints and marrow, and able to judge the thoughts and intentions of the heart. (Hebrews 4:12)

By the Word of God, Christians can put Satan to flight. Be sure to speak or read the Word *out loud*. Remember, Satan cannot read your thoughts. Demons will need to hear the word from your mouth before they will understand and obey what God is commanding them to do.

> Submit therefore to God. Resist the devil and he will flee from you. (James 4:7)

The sword of the Word of God is different from any other type of sword. A *material* sword is used with physical and mental power. The sword of the Spirit is the Spirit of God's sword and He must train us and give us the ability to use His Word properly and effectively. The Word is taught and brought to remembrance by the Holy Spirit.

> But the Helper, the Holy Spirit, whom the Father will send in My name, He will teach you all things, and bring to your remembrance all that I said to you. (John 14:26)

The Spirit resides in believers and enables us to understand and minister the Word. The teacher and administrator of the Word must be the Holy Spirit and not the flesh.

No physical or intellectual ability has anything to do with success in spiritual warfare.

> For though we walk in the flesh, we do not war according to the flesh, for the weapons of our warfare are not of the flesh, but divinely powerful for the destruction of fortresses. (2 Corinthians 10:3-4)

It is the authority and power of the Lord that sends malignant spirits running.

Many will say to Me on that day, 'Lord, Lord, did we not prophesy in Your name, and in Your name cast out demons, and in Your name perform many miracles?' And then I will declare to them, 'I never knew you; depart from Me, you who practice lawlessness.' (Matthew 7:22-23)

The power is the Word of God spoken in the power of the Spirit. If the Spirit does not control us, we will not use the Word of God as it is intended. It is the Spirit that makes the sword invincible in battle.

PERSONAL APPLICATION

1) Why were soldiers trained in using their sword? Why did they practice with it frequently?

2) Why do you need to be trained to use the Word of God and use it daily?

3) What three rebuttals did Jesus answer Satan in the wilderness in Matthew 4:1-11? Give Scripture reference for each.

4) Can you use the Word of God anyway you want? Who is to train us in the Word and teach us how to use it properly? Who is to be in control of the interpretation of God's Word?

5) Can Satan read our thoughts? When coming against Satan, why is it important to memorize Scripture and to speak Scripture out loud instead of *thinking* Scripture in our minds?

6) Which pieces of the armor are for defense? Which pieces are for offense? How will you apply and implement each piece of the armor in your life today?

Spiritual Warfare

25

SPIRITUAL STRONGHOLDS

For though we walk in the flesh, we do not war according to the flesh, for the weapons of our warfare are not of the flesh, but divinely powerful for the destruction of fortresses. We are destroying speculations and every lofty thing raised up against the knowledge of God, and we are taking every thought captive to the obedience of Christ, and we are ready to punish all disobedience, whenever your obedience is complete.
(2 Corinthians 10:3-6)

God wants us to know Him fully, and He wants nothing in the way of this closest of relationships. Our fallen or national patterns of thought and behavior keep us bound from fully thinking about and doing the ministry of God. But God has empowered believers to tear down anything that keeps us from fully knowing Him. Do you have thoughts that side-track or weaken your relationship with God and service for Him? Do those thoughts cause you anxiety or frustration? Do they hinder your prayer life and your understanding of the Bible? In 2 Corinthians 10:3-6,

Paul teaches how Christians can tear down debilitating old habits and thought patterns that assail and thwart us in our attempt to move closer to God.

The Corinthians judged Paul and his ministry by outward appearances and completely missed the spiritual power that was operating within him. They evaluated Paul and his activities according to the flesh and not according to the Spirit. But Paul was not walking or living according to the *natural* man as he had done prior to his conversion. He now walked in the Spirit and was relying solely on the *divine*. And because Paul walked in the Spirit, he developed weapons that were *spiritual*. Likewise, a follower of Christ cannot continue to allow his conduct to be controlled by the considerations of expediency or to allow his life to be focused on activities that are self-seeking. These are characteristic of the former unregenerated state when one is walking according to the flesh.

Though Paul does not fight according to the flesh, he does fight. He even admits that he leads an army to war. (The term war, *stratos*, literally means to "lead an army.") This war, though, was not against flesh and blood.

> Finally, be strong in the Lord and in the strength of His might. Put on the full armor of God, so that you will be able to stand firm against the schemes of the devil. For our struggle is not against flesh and blood, but against the rulers, against the powers, against the world forces of this darkness, against the spiritual forces of wickedness in the heavenly places.
> (Ephesians 6:10-12)

Paul's foes were the devil and his demonic agents, and what they were doing. He battled or "warred" against the powers of darkness by using *spiritual* weapons because you cannot fight spiritual battles with fleshly weapons. We too must put on the full armor of God and fight with spiritual weapons. For the Christian life is not merely a walk but also warfare (1 Timothy 1:18, 2 Timothy 2: 3-4, 2 Timothy 4:7, and 2 Corinthians 6:7).

A Christian who engages in warfare or a spiritual campaign must have the proper weapons with which to fight. Anyone can use *fleshly* weapons but too few in Christian circles can use *spiritual* weapons.

> Put on the full armor of God, so that you will be able to stand firm against the schemes of the devil. For our struggle is not against flesh and blood, but against the rulers, against the powers, against the world forces of this darkness, against the spiritual forces of wickedness in the heavenly places. Therefore, take up the full armor of God, so that you will be able to resist in the evil day, and having done everything, to stand firm. Stand firm therefore, having girded your loins with truth, and having put on the breastplate of righteousness, and having shod your feet with the preparation of the gospel of peace; in addition to all, taking up the shield of faith with which you will be able to extinguish all the flaming arrows of the evil one. And take the helmet of salvation, and the sword of the Spirit, which is the word of God. With all prayer and petition pray at all times in the Spirit, and with this in view, be on the alert with all perseverance and petition for all the saints... (Ephesians 6:11-18)

The armor of King Saul, though splendid in the eyes of men, cannot overcome the spiritual giants who come against us. Our most powerful opponents are not flesh and blood foes.

Attempting to withstand them with fleshly weapons would be a great folly.

We need divinely powerful weapons. We need weapons that are made mighty by God. Paul's attitude of humility is one weapon since pride places us in the control of Satan (1 John 2:15; James 4:4-10; Jeremiah 49:16; Daniel 5:20). Spiritual weapons like the Lordship of Christ, the Word of God, prayer, praise, love, peace, forgiveness, the sinless life, the perfect obedience of Christ, the Cross, the shed blood of the cross, the resurrection, and the ascension are a few of the weapons that defeat the enemy of our soul. Only spiritual weapons are divinely empowered for overthrowing the fortresses of evil.

There is a temptation to use fleshly weapons of human wisdom and strength when we come upon a person who is under the sway of the evil one, but that is not where true victory lies. Those who find and learn how to use *God's spiritual weapons*, in the power of God's Holy Spirit are empowered by God Himself for the destruction of strongholds in their life, in the life of their loved ones, their church, and in their community in which they battle. When engaging the enemy with these weapons, the church is assured of victory.

> For the word of the cross is foolishness to those
> who are perishing, but to us who are being
> saved it is the power of God.
> (1 Corinthians 1:18)

The world ignores or scorns God's spiritual weapons and wants to provoke you to use *fleshly* weapons. But when we turn to human methods, we find ourselves defeated by demonic forces. When Joshua and his army marched around

Jericho for a week, the spectators thought them mad. But the weapon of obedience to God's Word brought down the high walls and the enemy was conquered (Joshua 6:1-20). These spiritually powerful weapons are the ones the powers of darkness most vehemently fight against and keep from being used because they are the only weapons by which they and their work can be torn down!

> We are destroying speculations and every lofty thing raised up against the knowledge of God, and we are taking every thought captive to the obedience of Christ... (2 Corinthians 10:5)

This verse demonstrates the destructive and constructive capacity of God's divinely empowered weapons. God's spiritual weapons destroy reasonings and arguments that stand against the knowledge of God. There are worldly reckonings, reasonings, speculations or thoughts that invade, permeate, and then lay siege to the mind. The Bible treats these as fortresses or strongholds that need to be destroyed. These reasonings are walls of resistance built up by demonic influence in the minds of people, and like the walls of Jericho, these must be pulled down. Are you aware of the mental bastions in your mind?

These strongholds are more precisely defined as belonging to the will and intellect of man. They are reasonings within man that oppose the truth of God's Word. The exalted proud mind, its conscious and subconscious workings, and the hardened selfish will are sources of fallen man's beliefs. These inner machinations will influence, if not determine, external conduct. Such deceived attitude and thought patterns can become strongholds that affect our presuppositions and philosophies regarding what we do or do not do. The proud human mind that sees the cross of Christ as foolishness is one example of a stronghold (1 Corinthians 1:18), but there are many more deceived reasonings within each of our minds where Satan has built up his fortress within our way of thinking. Christian warfare is aimed at pulling down these proud reasonings, these rationalizations of self-centered man, these unyielding bulwarks within each of us that stand against our closer relationship to God. These strongholds have been repeatedly fortified by the lies of Satan that we have believed. And professing to be wise, we have exchanged the truth of God for a lie.

> For the wrath of God is revealed from heaven against all ungodliness and unrighteousness of men who suppress the truth in unrighteousness, because that which is known about God is evident within them; for God made it evident to them. For since the creation of the world His invisible attributes, His eternal power and divine nature, have been clearly seen, being understood through what has been made, so that they are without excuse. For even though they knew God, they did not honor Him as God or give thanks, but they became futile in their speculations, and their foolish heart was darkened. Professing to be wise, they became fools, and exchanged the glory of the incorruptible God for an image in the form of corruptible man and of birds and four-footed animals and crawling creatures. Therefore God gave them over in the lusts of their hearts to impurity, so that their bodies would be dishonored among them. For they exchanged the truth of God for a lie, and worshiped and served the creature rather than the Creator, who is blessed forever. Amen. (Romans 1:18-25)

Not only can we pull down these centers of obstruction against divine truth, but spiritually powerful weapons can also use them to capture or subdue every thought to the obedience of Christ. After storming, pulling down, and destroying these lofty high towers, we can take possession of them. These rebellious thoughts, preconceptions, and intentions can be made captive and brought into obedience to Christ. The obedience of Christ is the only stronghold that the enemy cannot enter into and conquer, therefore that is a fortress we desperately need in our life. Oh, that rebellion in our heart and mind might be quelled, and God's divine and sovereign will be made to reign in its place!

> ...and we are ready to punish all disobedience, whenever your obedience is complete.
> (2 Corinthians 10:6)

How do you know if you have torn down Satan's strongholds in your life, and are fortifying your life in obedience to Christ? Verse 6 explains. We will be ready to punish all disobedience, whenever your obedience is complete.

Once you have torn down known strongholds in your life and taken your will and thoughts captive for Christ, you become ready to punish or put to death all that is *not of Christ* in your life. As we grow in God's love and truth, we will always discover places that are still not in line with His Word. When these thoughts and actions raise their ugly head, we must relentlessly jump on them for we realize what would happen if they were to again gain a beachhead in our lives. Complete obedience means that we will not tolerate disobedience in our lives.

If you find that your thinking is not consistent with full obedience to Christ, then pride or sin could be deceiving you. It could be time for you to cast out anything in your life, *not of Him*. Fight the good fight of faith with divinely empowered weapons with Christ as your commander-in-chief. Put on God's full armor and come against those strongholds with the spiritual weapons of God. Continue in fervent, believing prayer until, by faith, you see those strongholds successfully torn down and destroyed. Then surrender yourself to be an instrument of righteousness with the newly conquered area spiritually activated (See Romans 6:5-23).

PERSONAL APPLICATION

1) List some fleshly weapons such as belittling, intimidation, gossip or false praise with which the world wars.

2) 2 Corinthians 10:3 reads, "For though we walk in the flesh, we do not war according to the flesh." Does our pride "keep us in" or "release us from" Satan's control?

3) Is anything in your mind usurping God's will, way, and Word? Is anything keeping you from knowing God more fully? Following Him more closely? Serving Him more faithfully?

4) What thoughts come up against you when you attempt to apply yourself to Christian teachings? What hinders your prayer life and the coherency of your Bible reading?

5) Do you have thoughts and actions that weaken your relationship with God and your service for Him? Ask God to reveal these areas to you. What are some powerful spiritual weapons or biblical truths that you can use to defeat the enemy?

26

THE ULTIMATE SPIRITUAL TASK

With all prayer and petition pray at all times in the Spirit, and with this in view, be on the alert with all perseverance and petition for all the saints, and pray on my behalf, that utterance may be given to me in the opening of my mouth, to make known with boldness the mystery of the gospel, for which I am an ambassador in chains; that in proclaiming it I may speak boldly, as I ought to speak.
(Ephesians 6:18-20)

After we have put on the spiritual armor, we are ready for battle. Living in the will of God and accomplishing His will certainly is a battle, but the battle is not only won or lost by praying, the battle *is* prayer. Satan will use his weapons to keep us from praying in the Spirit for prayer places us at the front lines of spiritual warfare where we can do damage to him and his kingdom. It is the ultimate weapon in the church's struggle "against the rulers, against the powers, against the world forces of this darkness, against the spiritual forces of wickedness in the heavenly places" (Ephesians 6:12). The "bent knee" is the absolute necessity in bringing victory to our spiritual battles because the Christian is totally dependent on help from above, which is secured through prayer.

The four "alls" in Ephesians 6:18 emphasizes the general characteristics of the believer's prayer life. We are to pray with all types of prayer, at all times, with all diligence, for all the saints. Prayer is of ultimate importance in the life of believers.

Prayer is the general term used in the New Testament for the prayers that Christians offer. In sections three and four of this book, entitled *Elements of Prayer*, the various types of prayer were discussed. Paul emphasizes the importance of using them all. There is no substitute for prayer. Extra efforts in service do not replace failure in our devotional life. You may attend Bible studies, participate in outreach, promote giving "and neglect the most vital part of your Christian experience—prayer. In our spiritual life, we can never rise above where we are in our prayer life. Prayerlessness is the foulest kind of humanism."[39]

Prayer is to be at all times and in the Spirit. It is not to be an *occasional activity* but engaged in *without ceasing*. There is no time of day, year, or life when we are *not* to pray. The Holy Spirit is to empower and guide both prayer and life. The Holy Spirit does not do one without the other. Prayer is to be an intense and reverent activity and not done with slack effort. There is a need for purpose and alertness in prayer. "Alert" or "watching" conveys the idea of staying awake to watch over someone or something.

> Be sober-minded; be watchful. Your adversary the devil prowls around like a roaring lion, seeking someone to devour. (1 Peter 5:8)

We are to persevere or give constant attention to alert praying. Though it is challenging and demanding, prayer is to be a continuous activity wholeheartedly undertaken by all believers.

The next instruction is that supplications are to be made for all the saints. The church is to be bound together by intercessions going up for one another. "No soldier entering battle prays for himself alone, but for all his fellow soldiers also. They form one army, and the success of one is the success of all."[40]

PERSONAL APPLICATION

1) Can you name the various types of prayers? (See Chapters 8 through 12.)

2) Where does prayer place us in this spiritual war against Satan and his demonic hordes?

3) What is the most vital and important event you can be involved in with your Christian service? Why is this true?

4) Are you assured that prayer is the most important ministry you render to God? Does the time you give prayer reflect that priority?

5) Why is supplication to be made for *all* the saints?

27

PRAYING THE PROMISES

Now Jabez called on the God of Israel, saying, "Oh that You would bless me indeed and enlarge my border, and that Your hand might be with me, and that You would keep me from harm that it may not pain me!" And God granted him what he requested.
(1 Chronicles 4:10)

One reason we pray weak prayers is that we do not "comprehend God's promises concerning the release of his supernatural power through prayer."[41] The promises of Scripture are the basis and motivation for prayer. They are the basis of prayer because they are God's guarantee that He will do or will not do certain acts. Prayer takes hold of God's promises and makes them personally real. Peter says the promises of God are precious and magnificent.

> For by these He has granted to us His precious and magnificent promises, so that by them you may become partakers of the divine nature,

having escaped the corruption that is in the world by lust. (2 Peter 1:4)

These promises motivate God's children and raise their expectation and confidence, as well as inspire and energize their praying to bring about God's glorious fulfillment. God's promises are the basis of faith and the solid ground of encouragement and inspiration. "Prayer must be based specifically upon God's revealed promises in Christ Jesus."[42] All the riches of God's promises come from and are found in Christ Jesus. There is no other basis upon which to plead God's promises.

One must claim God's promises to appropriate them. A general promise is not made to a specific person but is simply waiting in Scripture for a person to call forth their inheritance. Other promises have specific conditions that must first be met in the life of the believer. Specific promises are appropriated by completing their conditions and then laying hold of them by faith in God's power to bring them to fruition. God's promises should be lifted up in supreme confidence. God is not a man that He should lie. The promises of God lay in wait for men and women to realize their need and express their dependency upon God to fulfill His Word. This dependency comes about as one walks in daily relationship with God. This relationship opens one's eyes and matures one's faith.

Look for God's promises in His Word. Lay claim on those promises through prayer so that Jesus may be glorified through their fulfillment. John Newton penned the lyrics to the song "Amazing Grace," and they speak concisely of God's promises.

The Lord has promised good to me,
His Word my hope secures;
He will my shield and portion be
As long as life endures.[43]

PERSONAL APPLICATION

1) Are the promises of God a basis of your praying? Why should they be?

2) Do the promises of God motivate you to pray?

3) What is the difference between a general promise and a conditional promise?

4) Why do you think God makes conditional promises?

5) Do you think the Holy Spirit could apply a Scripture promise to you that was originally made to someone else?

Being United in Prayer

28

UNITY IN PRAYER

For their sakes I sanctify Myself, that they themselves also may be sanctified in truth... that they may all be one; even as You, Father, are in Me and I in You, that they also may be in Us, so that the world may believe that You sent Me. The glory which You have given Me I have given to them, that they may be one, just as We are one; I in them and You in Me, that they may be perfected in unity, so that the world may know that You sent Me, and loved them, even as You have loved Me.
(John 17:19, 21-23)

Amos proclaimed in Amos 3:3, "Can two walk together unless they agree?" Where there is unity of God's people with the Holy Spirit of God, there is an opportunity for God's great blessings. "Boiled down to its essence, unity means agreement"[44] As we unify to worship the Lord in Spirit and in truth, God responds with His blessed presence. When there is unity in the essential doctrines of the church, there is a closing of the ranks that forces out divisiveness.

> Therefore I, the prisoner of the Lord, implore you to walk in a manner worthy of the calling with which you have been called, with all humility and gentleness, with patience, showing tolerance for one another in love, being diligent to preserve the unity of the Spirit in the bond of peace. There is one body and one Spirit, just as also you were called in one hope of your calling; one Lord, one faith, one baptism, one God and Father of all who is over all and through all and in all. (Ephesians 4:1-6)

Where there is unity concerning the purpose of the church and being on mission to accomplish that purpose, the very gates of hell are broken open.

> I also say to you that you are Peter, and upon this rock I will build My church; and the gates of Hades will not overpower it. (Matthew 16:18)

When we join together to glorify God by carrying out the purpose of the church, the power of God moves His church forward.

In the verses from John, Chapter 17, we have part of Jesus' plea with the Father on behalf of His followers, the church. This section of the prayer was a plea for oneness of His body so that their testimony, of and for Jesus, might convince the world of its truthful reality. When we as a local church behave with divisiveness, discord, disharmony, and distrust we erode the validity that Jesus Christ is indeed the Son of God who gave His life to redeem man.

The power that sanctifies Jesus' disciples is the truth—the Word of God (John 17:17). As the truth has its effect in believers they become one. This oneness is emphasized by the striking similarity between John 17, verses 21 and 23.

...that they may all be one; even as You, Father, are in Me and I in You, that they also may be in Us, so that the world may believe that You sent Me. (John 17:21)

I in them and You in Me, that they may be perfected in unity, so that the world may know that You sent Me, and loved them, even as You have loved Me. (John 17:23)

The analogy is that the Father is *in* the Son and the Son is *in* the Father, making the two one essence, yet distinct. It should be so with believers who have Christ Jesus abiding in them. Those whom Christ abides within are to be unified by Christ to God and to each other as they are being sanctified by the truth. If they are unified, "The world may believe!" Unified disciples reflect the glory of Christ to the world. The purpose of manifesting God's glory in His disciples is to bring about unity. This spiritual unity of Christ's disciples then bears witness to the world that Jesus is real. The glory of Christian unity also manifests to the world what God's love is, because it is only in spiritual unity that God's love can truly be seen by the world.

PERSONAL APPLICATION

1) What is sanctification?

2) What is God's means of sanctifying His disciples?

3) What is an affect of the sanctification of believers?

4) Does the Son indwell believers? How does the world know the Son indwells believers?

5) What happens when believers are unified spiritually?

6) Which disciples reflect the glory of God to the world?

7) Was Jesus concerned that His people evangelize the world? How do you know that from John 17:21-23?

29

AGREEMENT IN PRAYER

"Again I say to you, that if two of you agree on earth about anything that they may ask, it shall be done for them by My Father who is in heaven. For where two or three have gathered together in My name, I am there in their midst." (Matthew 18:19-20)

Special blessings are promised by Jesus to those who meet in His name to find God's will and agree in prayer that it should be done. Public prayer brings up a great flourishing of fruitfulness, while private prayer helps one learn to sink their roots down deep into God.

> But you, when you pray, go into your inner room, close your door and pray to your Father who is in secret, and your Father who sees *what is done* in secret will reward you. (Matthew 6:6)

Prayer is developed in private communion and enhanced in public fellowship.

Within these verses of Matthew 18:19-20 are the indicators of true unified prayer. The first is that the prayer group has gathered together in Jesus' name. Jesus and His glory must be the reason they have gathered. He is the one who bonds believers together and makes them one in Him and in purpose. To gather in Jesus' name is to gather together to represent Jesus and to ask in accordance with His character and will. You can tell if a prayer group is gathered together to seek God's will and further the Kingdom of God because Jesus is in their midst and there is a special awareness of the living presence of Jesus among the group.

A complementary or perhaps a prerequisite indicator of true united prayer is unity or agreement. The Greek word for "agree" (συμφωνήσωσιν) is the origin of our word *symphony*. It means to produce a unified sound together. Each believer is to be an instrument in God's hands, under His direction. They are unified together by the Holy Spirit to follow His orchestration and not their own. As they are united together, God brings deep compassion, desire, or burden upon one, and the Holy Spirit transmits it as a consensus of His will to all. If the prayer is from selfish motivation, there will be no Spirit-led agreement.

The third indicator of unified prayer is that believers are able to obtain answers. The promise for those in agreement, who are praying in Jesus' name, is that "it shall be done for them by My Father who is in heaven." The fellowship and communion of brothers and sisters dwelling together in harmony may be sweet, but the purpose is securing answers to specific prayer. A prayer gathering should consistently realize answers to prayer. Who knows what great and mighty things God might presently be doing if united churches and small united prayer groups were gathering together in Jesus' name to advance His Kingdom on Earth?

PERSONAL APPLICATION

1) What are three evidences of true united prayer?

2) What is the over-arching purpose for those who have gathered in Jesus' name?

3) What does God promise will occur when two or three are gathered together in Jesus' name?

4) Is "agreement" to be first a consensus of minds or of the Spirit? What is the grand result of "Agreeing in Prayer?"

5) Do you pray regularly in Jesus' name with a small group? Would you be willing to join a small group and do so? Would you be willing to start a small group? If so, who are you going to ask to join you?

30

A HOUSE OF PRAYER

And He began to teach and say to them, "Is it not written, 'My house shall be called a house of prayer for all the nations?' But you have made it a robbers' den."
(Mark 11:17)

The following email crossed my desk:

We are sorry to announce the passing of Mrs. Prayer Meeting. She died recently at the First Neglected Church on Ho-Hum Avenue. Born many years ago, fed largely on testimony and Bible study, she grew into worldwide prominence and was one of the most influential members of the Church family. However, in recent years Sister Prayer Meeting has been failing in health, gradually wasting away until rendered helpless by stiffness of the knees, cooling of the heart, lack of spiritual sensitivity and the lack of concern for spiritual things. Her last whispered words were inquiring about the strange absence of her loved ones, now so busy in the market place and places of worldly amusement which have replaced prayer times!

Experts, including Dr. Good Works, Dr. Socializing and Dr. Unconcerned disagree as to the fatal cause of her final illness. They all administered large doses of excuses even ordered a last-minute motivational bypass, all to no avail. A post-mortem examination showed that a deficiency of regular spiritual food, a lack of prayer, and Christian fellowship all contributed to her untimely demise.

God's house is the place we come to meet God. There is no better way to encounter God than in prayer. Prayer addresses God and is our expression of wanting to meet with Him. God's house is where His presence is manifested in a special way. We should not be so concerned with people's presence in God's house as we are with God's presence in His house. In an organized church we are far too interested in attendance which has little if anything to do with God's presence. We certainly should be concerned about people, but large crowds do not equal a relationship with Christ. It is clear from Jesus' quotation that the Father's house is intended to be a place where God meets with His people. God set His house aside as a place for prayer and devotion.

We come to God's house to seek God. When God's people join together to seek God, He will be found. Many people come to church with the attitude of observing or attending and consequently get little out of it. If God's people join together to seek God, they will find Him and can express their devotion to Him. They may thank Him for all He is doing and ask Him to do what He so desires to do through them and through His church.

Jesus' action of cleansing the temple brought the crowd to attention, affording Him the opportunity to teach what Scripture says is to be the purpose of His house. In those days, worshippers entered the temple to seek the Divine Presence and found themselves in the midst of an uproar. The House of God is to be a place for God's glory, not used for the transaction of normal matters of life or business. All the commotion and activity of the day kept the Temple from being a place of prayer and devotion.

Jesus "began to teach and say to them 'Is it not written?'" And *it is written* in Isaiah 56:7 where the Word indicates that though they professed reverence for the Word of God, they habitually ignored it.

> Even those I will bring to My holy mountain
> And make them joyful in My house of prayer.
> Their burnt offerings and their sacrifices will be acceptable on My altar;
> For My house will be called a house of prayer for all the peoples." (Isaiah 56:7)

Jesus' statement, "For My house will be called a house of prayer for all the peoples" is His powerful incentive and endorsement for Christian missions.

> Also concerning the foreigner who is not of Your people Israel, when he comes from a far country for Your name's sake (for they will hear of Your great name and Your mighty hand, and of Your outstretched arm); when he comes and prays toward this house, hear in heaven Your dwelling place, and do according to all for which the foreigner calls to You, in order that all the peoples of the earth may know Your name, to fear You, as do Your people Israel, and that they

may know that this house which I have built is called by Your name. (1 Kings 8:41-43)

Go therefore and make disciples of all the nations, baptizing them in the name of the Father and the Son and the Holy Spirit, teaching them to observe all that I commanded you; and lo, I am with you always, even to the end of the age." (Matthew 28:19-20)

The Jews' misuse of God's house indicated a total indifference to winning the Gentiles to the Lord. We dare not also misuse God's house by not joining together in unity to pray for the salvation of the nations. God's house is to be a place for the upholding, strengthening, encouraging, and praising of God for the Christian missionary enterprise.

PERSONAL APPLICATION

1) Why do you go to God's house? Why do you think the average church member goes to God's house?

2) Do you encounter God's presence in your church?

3) Do you think the people of the church are more pleased with good attendance or with God's presence?

4) Why do you think Jesus quoted Scripture to the people?

5) What role do the people in God's house play in reaching the nations with the gospel of Jesus Christ?

6) Do you pray regularly for missionaries? Who are some of the missionaries you pray for?

7) Do you pray for the salvation of nations? Have you ever chosen a particular nation to pray for over a period of time?

8) How can your church do better at fulfilling the task of being a House of Prayer for the nations? What role can you play in fulfilling this need?

Conclusion

I trust that this journey into prayer has been worthwhile to you. You are to be commended for having taken it.

Boldly I pray that it has not simply been informative, but that it has been life-changing. God uses prayer to change the world, but first He uses it to change the one who is praying. Such transformation is rarely easy.

Nothing of significant, lasting value was ever accomplished without a commitment of the will. Once the commitment is made, persistence becomes essential. Commitment to perseverance in prayer is necessary if the skill of prayer is ever to be mastered. Without the commitment that leads to practice, a Christian will not become a person who executes transformative prayer. Without perseverance, the necessary level of practicing prayer that can radically change one's life or the lives of others, will not be attained.

Determine to practice and persevere in prayer, because without prayer all effort is of human strength and only brings temporary results because it has not secured God's involvement. It has wisely been said that until we pray, we do nothing of eternal value and after we pray, we can do all things.

Will you pray *without ceasing*?

NOTES

Chapter 3   The Spirit in Prayer

1. Murray, *Ministry of Intercession*, 97.
2. Ibid., 97.
3. R.A. Torrey, *How To Pray* (Chicago: Moody Press 1959), 53.
4. E. M. Bounds, *The Weapon of Prayer* (Grand Rapids: Baker Book House, 1931), 40.

Chapter 4   Getting Alone with God

5. J. Oswald Sanders, *Prayer Power Unlimited* (Chicago: Moody Press, 1977), 32, 33.
6. Thomas A. Kempis, *Of the Imitation of Christ* (Springdale, PA: Whitaker House, 1981), 43.
7. A. W. Tozer, *Man: the Dwelling Place of God* (Harrisburg, PA: Christian Publication, 1966), 9.
8. Brother Lawrence, *The Practice of the Presence of God* (Springdale, PA: Whitaker House, 1982), 15.

Chapter 5   Listening to God's Voice

9. Andrew Murray, *With Christ in the School of Prayer* (Old Tappen, NJ: Fleming H. Revell Company, 1953), 122.
10. Andrew Murray, *The Believer's Prayer Life* (Minneapolis: Bethany House Publishers, 1983), 91.

Chapter 6 Consistency with God

11. Psalms 5:3; 55:16,17; 78:34; 88:13; 90:14; Lamentations 3:22-24.
12. Mark 1:35; Matthew 14:23; Luke 15:16; 6:12.
13. Hunt, Doctrine, 122.
14. Murray, *The Believer's Prayer Life*, 79.

Chapter 7 The Prayer Notebook & Journaling

15. Taylor, 114,115.
16. Avery Willis, Jr., *MasterLife Discipleship Training, Vol. II.* (Nashville: Sunday School Board of the Southern Baptist Convention, 1980, 1982), 73.
17. Waylon B.Moore, *Living God's Word: Practical Lessons for Applying Scriptures* (Nashville: LifeWay Press, 1997), 58.
18. Ibid. 58.
19. Bill Hybel, *Too Busy Not to Pray* (Downers Grove, IL: InterVarsity Press, 1988, 1998G. R.), 130.
20. Elmer Towns, *Fasting For Spiritual Break Through* (Ventura, CA: Regal, 1996), 218.
21. Hybel, *Too Busy Not to Pray* (Downers Grove, IL: InterVarsity Press, 1988, 1998), 129.

Chapter 8 Adoration

22. Hunt, Doctrine, 50.
23. Merrill C. Tenney, ed. *The Zondervan Pictorial Encyclopedia of the Bible*, vol. 4, Prayer, by G. R. Lewis (Grand Rapids: The Zondervan Corporation, 1975), 839.

Chapter 9 Confession

24. J. Oswald Sanders, *Prayer Power Unlimited* (Chicago: Moody Press, 1977), 22.

Chapter 10 Thanksgiving

25. Sanders, 15.
26. John Bisagno, *The Power of Positive Praying* (Grand Rapids: Zondervan Publishing House, 1965), 49.
27. R. A. Torrey, *How to Pray* (Chicago: Moody Press, 1959), 71.
28. Examples can be found in Ephesians 5:20; Philippians 1:3; Colossians 1:3; 3:17; 1 Thessalonians 1:2; 5:18; 2 Thessalonians 1:3.
29. Hunt, Doctrine, 54.

Chapter 11 Intercession

30. Andrew Murray, *The Ministry of Intercession* (Springdale, PA: Whitaker House, 1982), 138-145.
31. Ibid., 142.

Chapter 13 Praying in Jesus' Name

32. Lehman Strauss, *Sense and Nonsense About Prayer* (Chicago: Moody Press, 1974), 38.

Chapter 14 Praying in Faith

33. Hybel, 84.

Chapter 16 Unanswered Prayers

34. Charles Stanley, *Handle With Prayer* (Colorado Springs: Victor Books, 1982, 1992), 63.
35. Ibid. 64.

Chapter 18 Spiritual Armor

36. John Piper, *Let the Nations Be Glad* (Grand Rapides: Baker Book House, 1993), 41.

Chapter 22 The Shield of Faith

37. John MacArthur. Ephesians. *MacArthur New Testament Commentary*. 1986 Moody Bible Institute: Chicago. P. 357.
38. John MacArthur, *How To Meet The Enemy* (Wheaton, IL: Victor Books, 1992), 112.

Chapter 26 The Ultimate Spiritual Task

39. Paul W. Powel, *The Great Deceiver* (Nashville: Broadman Press, 1988), 117.
40. Charles Hodge, *Commentary on the Epistle to the Ephesians* (Grand Rapids: Eermans Publishing Co., 1994), 392.

Chapter 27 Praying the Promises

41. Stanley, *Handle With Prayer*, 110.
42. E. M. Bounds, *The Possibilities of Prayer* (Grand Rapids: Baker Book House, 1979), 22.
43. Joe Aldrich, *Reunites* (Sister, OR: Multnomah Books, 1992, 1994), 100.

Chapter 28 Unity in Prayer

44. Jim Cymbala, *Fresh Faith* (Grand Rapids: Zondervan Publishing House, 1999), 37.

ABOUT CLIMBING ANGEL PUBLISHING

Climbing Angel Publishing exists for the purpose of sharing stories of hope and encouragement, aiding in the gathering together of community, and supporting the process of betterment. The following books are available at ClimbingAngel.com and major bookstores.

Adult Books: *(Romans 8:28-30)*

In His Image
By Faith
Without Ceasing

Children's Books: *(Philippians 4:8)*

The Christmas Tree Angel
The Unmade Moose
Thump
Somebunny To Love

Learning to be a PRAYER WARRIOR is a JOURNEY

Strengthen this ability in a group!

Without Ceasing is available at a discount for small groups and church-wide initiatives.

Order direct from Climbing Angel Publishing by emailing:

ClimbingAngel Publishing@gmail.com

Grow into the likeness of Christ with Sam Polson's *IN HIS IMAGE!*

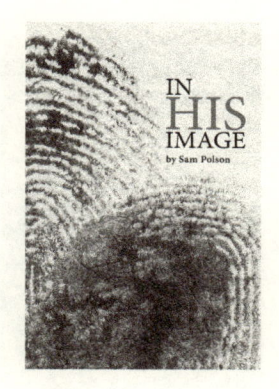

"I challenge you to read and grow into the likeness of our Creator and Redeemer. *In His Image* will inspire, educate, and guide you in that sacred process." — Rev. Sam Phillips

"In a culture awash with self-identity talk, Pastor Sam Polson directs us to the truest identity of all... the Lord Jesus Christ Himself." — Dr. Greg Baker

"*In His Image* is a book I highly recommend to assist in family worship, private devotion, or person study." — Dr. David Trempe

Available in:
English (ISBN: 978-0-99657-219-4)
Romanian (ISBN: 978-0-99657-218-7)
Chinese (ISBN: 978-1-64370-036-6)
www.climbingangel.com

Learn of the *Timeless Value* of Hebrews, Chapter 11
in Sam Polson's *BY FAITH*

"*By Faith* will be a helpful addition to the library of any serious Bible student." — Dr. Steve Euler

"Through *By Faith* you will be encouraged by the heart, the hope, and the wisdom that has encouraged my journey for almost two decades."
— Pastor Rick Dunn

"Sam Polson...leads the believer down a path, living out their faith practically, in clear and logical steps. You will be blessed!"
— Pastor Mark Kirk

Available in:
English (ISBN: 978-1-64370-035-9)
Romanian (ISBN: 978-1-64370-032–8)
www.climbingangel.com

CPSIA information can be obtained
at www.ICGtesting.com
Printed in the USA
LVHW030541170519
618165LV00001B/1/P

9 781643 700335